A Bevy of BASKETS

Carole Wells   Sandra Jordan

This book is dedicated to:

BILL WELLS

PAIGE WELLS

JILL WELLS

TOM WELLS

and

LEE TOLLESON JORDAN

Photography by Carole Hunt Wells
Illustrations by Sandra Long Jordan
Calligraphy by Sharon McLamb

Library of Congress Catalog Number: 86-72340
ISBN: 0-9617472-0-X

Second Printing - 1987

Printed in the United States of America

CRAFTER'S PRESS
P. O. Box 971
Smithfield, North Carolina
27577

TABLE OF CONTENTS

ACKNOWLEDGMENTS

We would like to express our appreciation to the following people who offered us encouragement and advice during the time we were developing this book.

The following people attended the workshops we held and proved that our patterns really would make a basket:

Debbie Whitley	Connie Smart	Kay Parrish
Kathy Batten	Lib Garris	Pat Byrd
Janice Dalfors	Gayle Bizzell	Joanne Brown
Priscilla Overby	Mary Humphrey	Shirley & Fred Mozingo
Clarisse Giddens	Betty Sambleson	

A special thanks goes to Myra Wallace who proofread the manuscript.

Our deepest appreciation goes to our typist, Priscilla Overby. Her knowledge of typing and basketry, as well as her endless enthusiasm, made her an invaluable asset in the completion of this book.

INTRODUCTION

Unlike many other crafts, basketry gives one the
satisfaction of creating something that is functional as well as
decorative. Many of the baskets included in this book are
reproductions of old baskets. Because of a difference in the
materials which have been used, they may not be suitable for
their original purposes. The baskets, which have been made using
commercial reeds, are not as strong as the old baskets made of
other materials. Some of the baskets have been reduced in size
so that they will retain some functional quality.

This book is divided into four sections according to the
different types of basket construction. Each section is arranged
with the easiest basket first. After developing the skills
taught in the first basket, each succeeding basket will reinforce
these skills and add to them. Each pattern gives step-by-step
instructions and illustrations where they are needed for clarity.
After completing a series of baskets, one should be able to make
unlimited variations by substituting materials and changing
dimensions.

BASKETRY TERMS

FRAME: The construction of every basket begins with its frame which determines what size the basket will be. Each type of basket depends upon a different technique for making the frames. Once constructed, weavers will be used to fill in the bottom and sides of the basket.

TWINING: Twining is a weaving technique which is used to secure the frame of some types of baskets. It is also a method used when weaving with round reed. There is an illustration of this technique in the section entitled, "Types of Weaves".

RIBS: Ribs are pieces of round reed which are inserted into the frame and form the shape of the basket.

SPOKES: Spokes, like ribs, are the foundation of certain baskets. They radiate from the center of the basket similar to the spokes in a bicycle tire.

STAKES: Stakes, like ribs and spokes, are the foundation of the plaited baskets.

WEAVER: A weaver is any reed which is used to fill in the frame of the basket.

ROUND: A round is the weaving of one row completely around the basket and back to its staring point.

PACKING: Packing is pushing the weavers tightly together as they are woven into the basket.

SPLICING: Splicing is the technique used to add a new weaver when the old one runs out.

RIM: The rim is the top of a finished basket.

GOD'S EYE: The God's Eye is a weaving techinque used to secure the frames of certain baskets.

TOOLS AND EQUIPMENT

The following items will be useful for making baskets.

TOWEL: Because the reeds must be dampened, a towel will be used for absorbing excess water and drying one's hands.

BUCKET: A large bucket or tub will be used to hold water for dampening the reeds.

SCISSORS, KNIFE, WIRE CUTTERS: These items, which should be kept sharpened, are used for cutting reeds, cord, and tape. A small pair of scissors is handy for reaching awkward places.

TAPE MEASURE: A flexible tape measure is best because it conforms to the shape being measured.

PENCIL SHARPENER: The pencil sharpener is used to sharpen the ends of reeds used in baskets of the ribbed-type cnstruction. A hand-held sharpener works well, but an electric one will do this job in a snap.

AWL, ICE PICK: These items will be used to open up spaces for the insertion of reeds.

MASKING TAKE, CORD, TWINE, CLOTHESPINS: These items will be useful as a third hand in holding parts of the basket temporarily in place while it is under construction.

DYEING BASKETRY MATERIALS

The reeds come in their natural buff color, but may be dyed if desired. Commercial dyes are easy to use and come in a variety of colors. Natural brown-toned dyes may be obtained by boiling nuts and bark of various trees; such as walnut, chestnut, and white oak. Other materials which may be used to stain the reeds are coffee, tea, and chewing tobacco. Commercial woodstains, which are water-soluble, may also be used.

TYPES OF WEAVES

TWINING

PLAIN WEAVE
(Over one, under one)

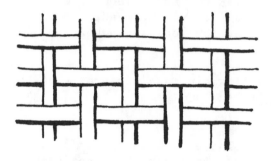

HERRINGBONE
(Over two, under two)

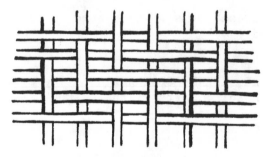

PLAIN WEAVE
(Using double strand)

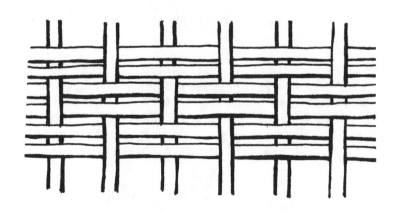

TYING OFF RIMS

Rims may be tied off using various materials and techniques. The style and size of a basket will determine which method is most suitable.

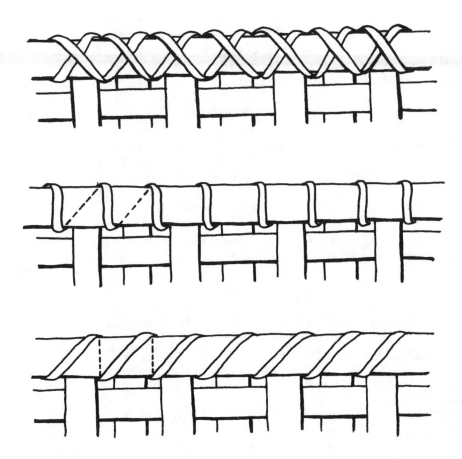

DESCRIPTION OF MATERIALS USED IN BASKETRY

FLAT REED

Flat reed is available in several widths. It is used in many baskets as both spokes and weavers. Commercial flat reed has a smooth and a rough side. The smooth side should be woven on the outside of the basket.

FLAT OVAL REED

Flat oval reed is available in several widths. It differs from flat reed in that one side is flat and the other is curved. The curved side is the top or outer side. It is used for weaving and for making rims on the tops of baskets.

ROUND REED

Round reed is sold in one pound coils. These reeds are used as weavers and spokes in various baskets. Available in a variety of sizes, this is also used to repair wicker furniture.

WOODEN HOOPS

Wooden hoops are used as frames for ribbed baskets. They are available in many sizes both round and oval.

CANE

Strand cane is used in handwoven seats and is sold in bundles of 1,000 feet. (It is available in several sizes.)

Binding cane is used to cover holes and give a finished look to the seat. It comes in bundles of 500 feet. This type of cane may be purchased in small amounts. This is available in 4mm, 5mm, and 6mm widths.

Both types of cane are used for tying off the tops of baskets. The width used depends on the size of the basket. The wider cane will be stronger and hold better on baskets made of heavy materials. The cane is glossy on one side and dull on the other. Either side may be turned outward.

Round Baskets

HELPFUL SUGGESTIONS FOR ROUND BASKETS

1. The bundles of reeds are referred to as hanks. Once a hank of reed is broken, it becomes difficult to handle. Because it is impractical to retie the hanks each time a few reeds are needed, a good method of storage is necessary. Plastic trash bags and old pillow cases are ideal for this purpose.

2. One side of a flat reed is smoother than the other. To find the smooth side, dampen the reed and bend it back and forth in your hands. When bent, the rough side has a splintered appearance. In order that the basket may be as neat as possible, always turn the reed so that the smooth side will be on the outside of the basket.

   > NOTE: If the inside of the basket will be more obvious, turn the smooth side of the reed to the inside.

3. Care should be taken when wetting the flat reeds. Too much water will cause the reed to fray and split. When a direction calls for "dampening", immerse the reed in water briefly, but do not allow it to soak. Excess water may be blotted from the reed with a towel.

4. It may be necessary to soak round reed for several minutes to insure that it will not break.

5. Any reeds which have been dampened, but not used, should be allowed to dry before being stored to prevent the growth of mildew.

6. Weave by bending the weavers around the spokes and placing them as close to the previous round as possible. Do not allow the weavers to bend the spokes. This bending will, most likely, occur at the beginning of the basket.

7. Most baskets have a flat bottom. An inexperienced basketmaker has a tendency to force the weavers into place causing the spokes to turn up too soon. The weavers need to be bent around the spokes allowing them to remain flat on the table.

   One way to eliminate this problem is, after a few rounds, turn the basket over and weave from the other side. Alternating the weaving in this manner may help to keep the bottom flat.

8. Clothespins are handy for securing reeds in place when making baskets. (Examples: attaching the rim, splicing new weavers, and holding the top round in place on large baskets.)

9. The bottom of an unlevel basket may be flattened by doing the following:

   A. Wet the bottom of the basket.
   B. Turn it upside down on a smooth surface.
   C. Place a heavy, flat object, such as an iron skillet on the basket until the reed has dried.

12

BREAD BASKET

Because of the simplicity of its construction, the bread basket is ideal for beginners. The size and shape of the basket make it suitable for serving breads, chips, and other snacks.

BREAD BASKET

Dimensions:
    Diameter of top: 9"
    Diameter of bottom: 6"
    Height: 3 3/4"

Materials:
    #2 round reed
    1/2" flat reed
    3/8" flat oval reed
    3/16" flat oval reed

TO MAKE THE BOTTOM:

1. Cut eight pieces of 1/2" flat reed 18" long. Mark the center of the rough side of each piece with a dot 9" from the end. These pieces of reed will be the spokes which form the framework of the basket.

2. Cut one piece of 1/2" flat reed 9" long.

3. Wet the spokes and place them, smooth side down, in the order shown in the illustration. Start with number one. Use the dots to center the spokes. Be sure to hide the end of the 9" spoke between the other spokes in the center.

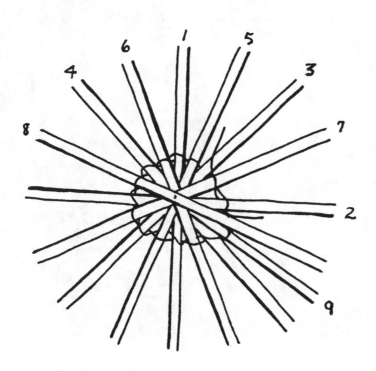

4. Using string, tie the spokes together by twining one round. Knot the string and cut off the excess. This string may be removed after the basket is completed.

5. Soak several strands of #2 round reed in warm water for five minutes.

6. Using one strand of round reed, begin weaving over one, under one, forming a circle 3 1/2" in diameter.

7. As you complete this circle and begin the second round, the round reed should be going over the spokes the reed went under on the first round, and going under the spokes it went over. This pattern should continue as you weave. If it does not, you have gone over two or under two, and you must go back and correct the mistake.

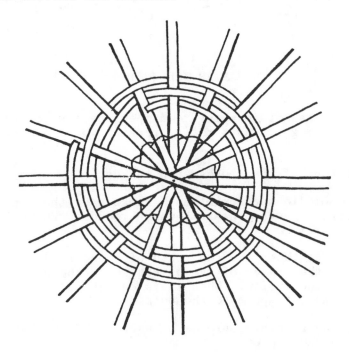

8. When the first weaver runs out, add another reed as shown in the illustration. This is called splicing. Continue adding new weavers, as necessary, using this method.

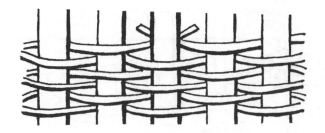

TO WEAVE THE SIDES:

9. When a circle 6" in diameter has been woven, wet the basket and bend the spokes up to form the sides. The bottom of the basket should be flat.

10. Continue weaving until the desired height of the basket is reached.

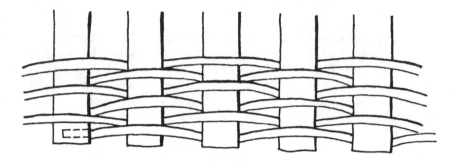

TO FINISH THE TOP:

11. Invert the basket in water to dampen the tops of the spokes. This dampening prevents their breaking when locking the top in place.

12. Cut the tops of the spokes into thirds.

13. Bend the middle section of each spoke over the top two rounds and insert it under the next three rounds. Cut off any excess.

    > NOTE: When the top round of round reed is on the inside of the basket, bend the spoke to the inside. When it is on the outside, bend the spoke to the outside.

14. Cut off the remaining pieces of each spoke so that they are even with the top of the basket.

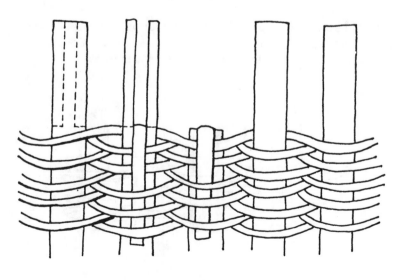

TO ATTACH THE RIM:

15. Cut two pieces of 3/8" flat oval reed 31" long for the outside and inside rims.

16. With the flat sides of the reed against the basket, place one on the inside top of the basket and one on the outside. Use clothespins to hold the rim in place.

> NOTE: Overlapping the ends of each piece on opposite sides of the basket will prevent the formation of an unsightly bulge on one side of the basket.

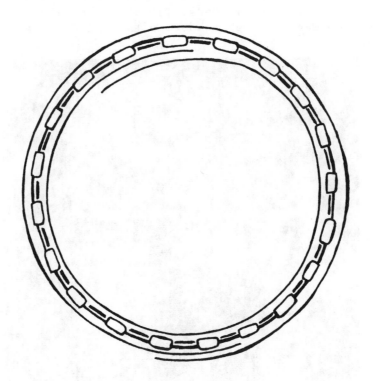

17. Using 3/16" flat oval reed, tie off the rim using any of the methods illustrated in the section entitled "Tying off Rims."

TALL, ODD-SHAPED BASKET

This basket looks nice on the floor holding an arrangement of dried flowers. If it is inclined to tip over. The bottom may be weighted down with a heavy object.

TALL, ODD-SHAPED BASKET

Dimensions:
    Diameter of top: 6"
    Diameter of bottom: 6"
    Height: 14"

Materials:
    1/2" flat reed
    1/4" flat reed
    7/8" flat oval reed
    3/16" flat oval reed

TO MAKE THE BOTTOM:

1. Cut eight pieces of 1/2" flat reed 40" long. Mark the center of the rough side of each piece with a dot 20" from the end. These pieces of reed will be the spokes which form the framework of the basket.

2. Cut one piece of 1/2" flat reed 20" long.

3. Wet the pieces of reed and arrange them, smooth side down, as shown in the illustration. Start with number one. Use the dots to center the spokes. Be sure to hide the end of the 20" spoke between the other spokes in the center.

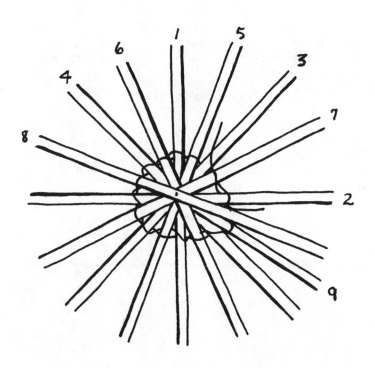

19

4. Using string, tie the spokes together by twining one round. Knot the string and cut off the excess. This string may be removed after the basket is completed.

5. Cut a piece of 1/4" flat reed lengthwise, using scissors, to make two pieces of 1/8" flat reed.

6. Using one piece of 1/8" flat reed, weave over one spoke and under one spoke to form a circle 3 1/2" in diameter.

7. As you complete this circle and begin the second round, the weaver should be going over the spokes it went under on the first round and under the spokes it went over. This pattern should continue as you weave. If it does not, you have gone over or under two spokes and must go back and correct the mistake.

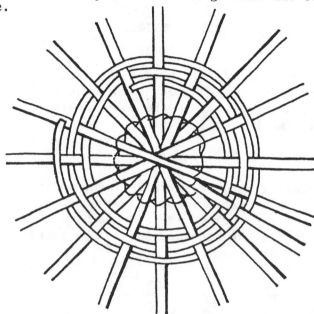

8. When the bottom of the basket is woven to a diameter of 6", begin pulling the weaver more tightly to gradually turn up the sides.

TO WEAVE THE SIDES:

9. As the sides turn up, begin weaving with 1/4" flat reed. Continue weaving until the sides of the basket are 13 1/2" tall. Pull the weaver even tighter near the top to bring in the sides.

10. At the end of each weaver, add a new piece of reed as shown in the illustration. Continue weaving as before.

> NOTE: Taper the last few inches of the top round for a better fitting rim.

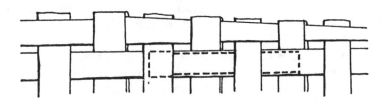

TO FINISH THE TOP:

11. Dampen the top of the basket and lock the spokes into place. The spokes on the outside of the top round should be cut so that they are 2" long. These spokes will be folded to the inside of the basket and tucked into the third weaver from the top as shown in the following illustration. Cut off the spokes on the inside of the basket so that they will be even with the top round.

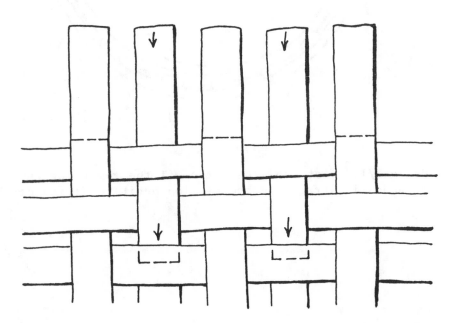

TO ATTACH THE RIM:

12. Cut two pieces of 7/8" flat oval reed 45" long for the outside and inside rims.

13. With the flat sides of the reed against the basket, place one on the inside top of the basket and one on the outside. Use clothespins to hold the rim in place.

> NOTE: Overlapping the ends of each piece on opposite sides of the basket will prevent the formation of an unsightly bulge on one side of the basket.

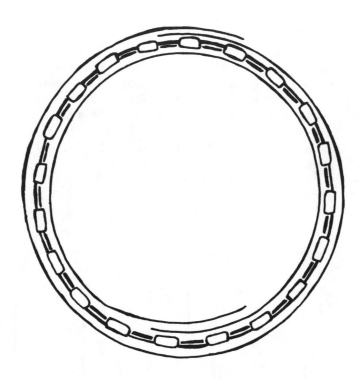

14. Using 3/16" flat oval reed, tie off the rim using any of the methods illustrated in the section entitled "Tying off Rims."

HANGING BASKET

As its name implies, this basket is meant to be
suspended from the ceiling or a bracket for hanging plants.

HANGING BASKET

Dimensions:
    Diameter of top: 8 1/2"
    Diameter of bottom: 5 1/2"
    Height: 5"

Materials:
    1/2" flat reed
    1/4" flat reed
    3/8" flat oval reed
    1/2" flat oval reed
    #2 round reed

TO MAKE THE BOTTOM:

1. Cut eight pieces of 3/8" flat reed 18" long. Mark the center
    of the rough side of each piece with a dot 9" from the end.
    Cut one piece of 3/8" flat reed 9" long. These pieces of
    reed will be the spokes which form the framework of the
    basket.

2. Wet the spokes and arrange them, smooth side down, as shown
    in the illustration. Be sure to hide the end of the 9" spoke
    between the other spokes in the center.

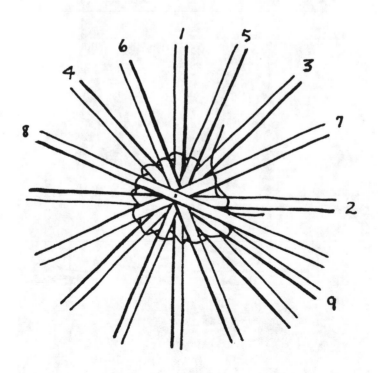

3. Using string, tie the spokes together by twining one round. Knot the string and cut off the excess. This string may be removed after the basket is completed.

4. Soak several strands of #2 round reed in warm water for five minutes.

5. Take one strand of round reed and weave over one spoke and under one spoke to form a circle 3 1/2" in diameter.

6. As you complete this circle and begin the second round, the round reed should be going over the spokes the reed went under on the first round, and going under the spokes it went over. This pattern should continue as you weave. If it does not, you have gone over two or under two, and your must go back and correct the mistakes.

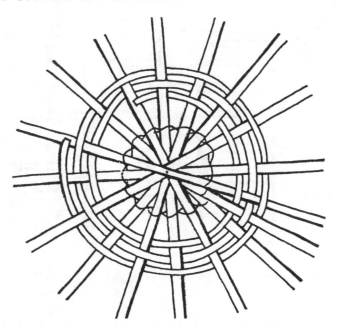

7. When the first weaver runs out, add another reed as shown in the illustration. This is called splicing. Continue adding new weavers, as necessary, using this method.

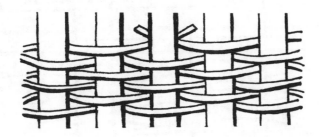

TO WEAVE THE SIDES:

8. Continue weaving until the bottom of the basket is 5 1/2" in diameter. As the weaving continues, pull the sides up gradually. After 2 1/2" have been woven, the sides should be standing up.

9. Using a piece of 3/8" flat oval reed, weave three rounds. Taper the ends of the reed 3" on each side so that it will blend into the round reed as shown in the illustration.

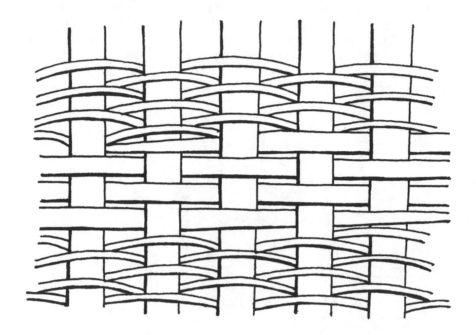

10. Using #2 round reed, continue weaving for 2 1/4".

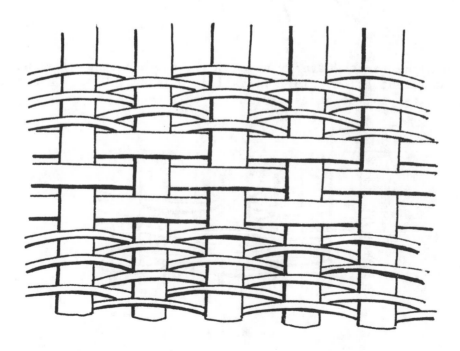

TO FINISH THE TOP:

11. Invert the basket in water to dampen the tops of the spokes. This dampening prevents their breaking when the top is being locked into place.

12. Cut the tops of the spokes into thirds.

13. Bend the middle section of each spoke over the top two rounds and insert it under the next three rounds. Cut off any excess.

> NOTE: When the top round of round reed is on the inside of the basket, bend the spoke to the inside. When it is on the outside, bend the spoke to the outside.

14. Cut off the remaining pieces of each spoke so that they are even with the top of the basket.

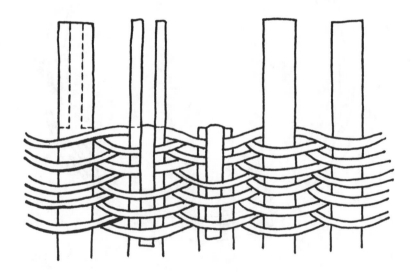

TO ATTACH THE RIM:

15. Cut two pieces of 3/8" flat oval reed 31" long for the outside inside rims.

16. With the flat sides of the reed against the basket, place one on the inside top of the basket and one on the outside. Use clothespins to hold the rim in place.

> NOTE: Overlapping the ends of each piece on opposite sides of the basket will prevent the formation of an unsightly bulge on one side of the basket.

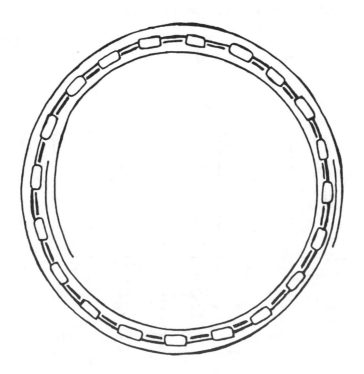

17. Using 3/16" flat oval reed, tie off the rim using any of the methods illustrated in the section entitled "Tying off Rims."

TO MAKE THE CHAIN:

18. Cut 34 pieces of #2 round reed 15" long.

19. Form a circle about 1 1/2" in diameter using one piece of the reed.

20. Loop one end around and inside of the circle until a link is formed.

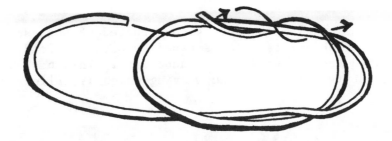

21. Insert another 15" reed through the link previously made. Follow the same procedure to make a second link.

22. Continue adding links until the chain is the desired length.

23. Make two more chains that are the same length as the first one.

24. Measure the top of the basket. Divide the measurement into thirds. Using this figure, divide the top of the basket into thirds and mark each point where the chains will be attached.

25. At each point which has been marked, the chain will be attached to the basket by adding a link which will be inserted through the end link and the rim of the basket.

26. Join the three chains, by adding a final link which will connect them at the top.

> NOTE: The chains alone are not strong enough to support a heavy planter. Wires or strong cord should be threaded through each link and attached to the planter as an additional means of support.

AUNT RUTH'S BASKET

The original basket is constructed of honeysuckle vine and white oak splits. It is owned by Sue Stanfield who inherited the basket from her Aunt Ruth. This basket uses a different technique for the weaving which is called twining.

AUNT RUTH'S BASKET

Dimensions:
    Diameter of top: 9"
    Diameter of bottom: 9"
    Height: 3 1/4"

Materials:
    #1 round reed   1/4" flat reed
    #2 round reed   3/8" flat oval reed
    1/2" flat reed   3/16" flat oval reed

TO MAKE THE BOTTOM:

1. Cut nine pieces of 1/2" flat reed 18" long. Mark the center of the rough side of each piece with a dot 9" from the end. These pieces of reed will be the spokes which form the framework of the basket.

2. Wet the spokes and place them, smooth side down, in the order shown in the illustration. Start with number one. Use the dots to center the spokes.

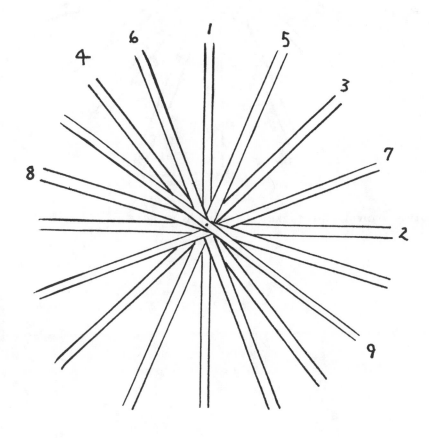

31

3. Using string, tie the spokes together by twining one round. Knot the string and cut off the excess. This string may be removed after the basket is completed.

4. Soak several strands of #1 round reed in warm water for five minutes.

5. Fold a strand of the round reed over and under one spoke as illustrated. Make certain that the ends are unequal in length so that both ends will not be spliced at the same place.

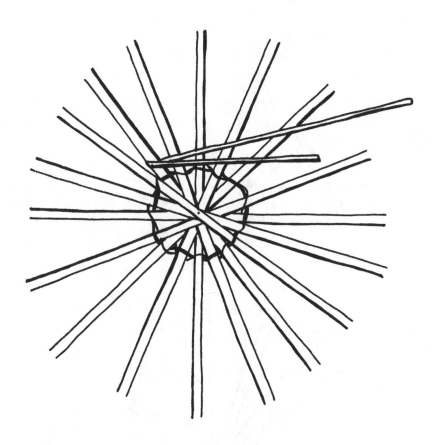

6. Twine around the spokes forming a circle 3 1/2" in diameter.

NOTE: Unlike the following illustration, each round must be woven tightly against the preceding one. Once in place, the twining technique cannot be packed closer to the center.

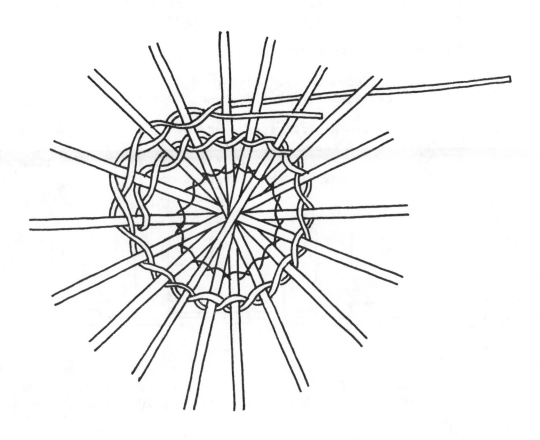

7. Dampen several strands of #2 round reed. Using this size reed, continue weaving until the circle is 9" in diameter.

TO WEAVE THE SIDES:

8. Dampen the bottom of the basket and bend the spokes up to form the sides. Using #2 round reed, twine up the sides one inch. To make the sides stay up, pull the weavers tightly.

9. Cut the following pieces of reed:

   > Two pieces of 1/2" flat reed 35" long
   > One piece of 1/4" flat reed 35" long

10. Using one piece of 1/2" flat reed, weave over one spoke and under one spoke until the weaver has been inserted all the way around the basket. Overlap the ends of the weaver and hide them behind the spokes as shown in the illustration.

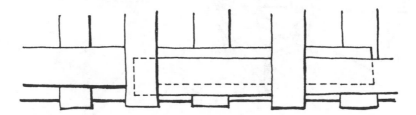

11. Using the 1/4" flat reed, weave over one and under one on the opposite spokes which were used in step 10. Overlap and hide the ends.

12. Repeat step 10.

13. Using a strand of dampened #2 round reed, fold it over and around a spoke and continue twining for 1 1/8" to complete the sides.

TO FINISH THE TOP:

14. Invert the basket in water to dampen the tops of the spokes. This dampening prevents their breaking when locking the top in place.

15. Cut the tops of the spokes so that each one is 1 1/2" long. Cut each spoke into thirds.

16. Bend the middle section of each spoke over the top two rounds of round reed and insert it under the next three rounds. Cut off any excess.

> NOTE: When the top round of round reed is on the inside of the basket, bend the spoke to the inside. When it is on the outside, bend the spoke to the outside.

17. Cut off the remaining pieces of each spoke so that they are even with the top of the basket.

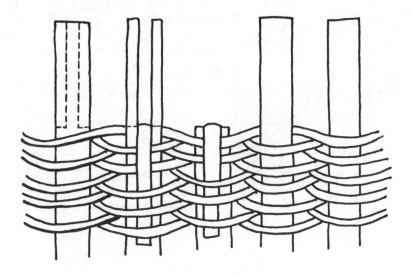

TO MAKE THE DECORATIVE CIRCLES:

18. Place the end of a dyed #2 round reed between an upper 1/2"
    weaver and a 1/2" spoke. Take the round reed down and over
    the 1/4" weaver. Go between the lower 1/2" weaver and 1/2"
    spoke and over the 1/4" weaver on the other side. Take the
    reed between the upper weaver and spoke where it was first
    inserted to complete one circle. Repeat this step twice
    more.

19. Skipping one spoke, take the dyed reed across the flat reed
    to the lower 1/2" weaver.

20. Repeat steps 18 and 19 until the decorative reed encircles
    every other spoke in the basket.

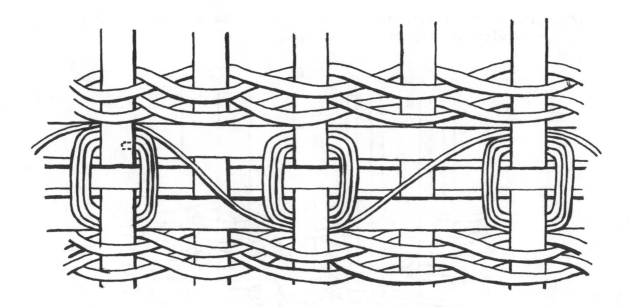

36

TO ATTACH THE RIM:

21. Cut two pieces of 3/8" flat oval reed 33" long for the outside and inside rims.

22. With the flat sides of the reed against the basket, place one on the inside top of the basket and one on the outside. Use clothespins to hold the rim in place.

> NOTE: Overlapping the ends of each piece on opposite sides of the basket will prevent the formation of an unsightly bulge on one side of the basket.

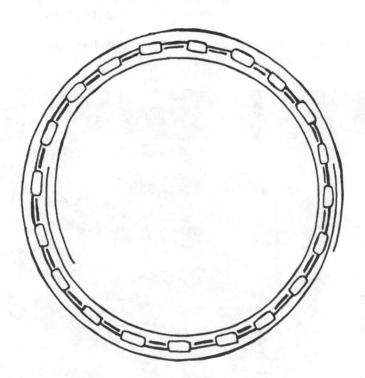

23. Using 1/4" flat reed or narrow cane, tie off the rim using any of the methods illustrated in the section entitled "Tying off Rims."

DECORATIVE FIELD BASKET

The field basket, which holds about one peck, may be used for gathering small amounts of vegetables.

The dyed material is used in the basket in such a way as to give the appearance of a chain.

DECORATIVE FIELD BASKET

Dimensions:
   Diameter of top: 12"
   Diameter of bottom: 12"
   Height: 9"

Materials:
   7/8" flat reed   7/8" flat oval reed
   1/2" flat reed   1/4" flat oval reed
   3/8" flat reed   3/16" flat oval reed

TO MAKE THE BOTTOM:

1. Cut eight pieces of 7/8" flat reed 32" long. Cut one piece of 7/8" flat reed 16" long. These reeds will be the spokes which form the framework of the basket.

2. Dampen the spokes.

3. Fold each 7/8" spoke in half and cut the center of each one as shown in the illustration.

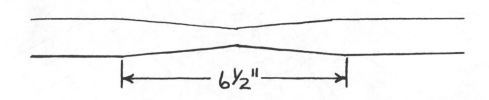

4. Cut one end of the 16" spoke so that it will fit in and look like the others.

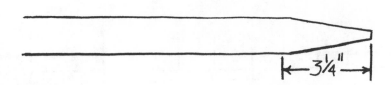

39

5. Dampen the spokes and arrange them, smooth side down, as shown in the illustration which follows. Start with #1. Be sure to hide the end of the 16" spoke between the other spokes in the center.

6. Using string, tie the spokes in place by twining one round. Knot the string and cut off any excess length. This string may be removed after the basket is completed.

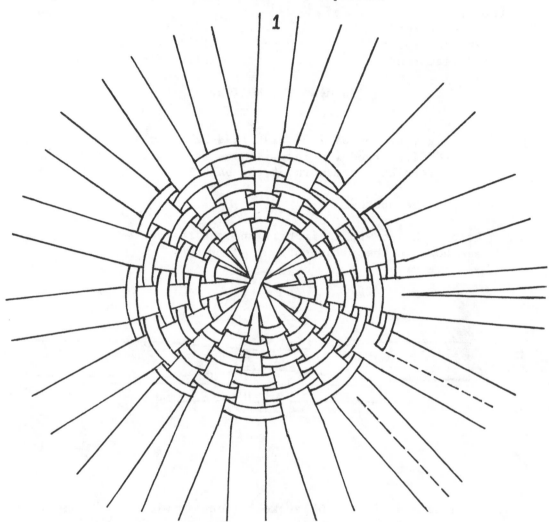

NOTE: At the end of each weaver, add a new piece of reed as shown in the illustration. Continue weaving as before.

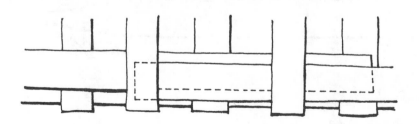

7. With the oval side out, begin weaving a strand of dampened 3/16" flat oval reed over one, under one, packing the weaver tightly against the center of the bottom. You can weave close to the center of the basket because of the tapered spokes.

8. Weave seven rounds or until you reach the end of the taper.

9. Cut each 7/8" spoke lengthwise making two spokes out of each one. Each new spoke will be 7/16" wide.

10. Using the 3/16" flat oval reed, weave until the spaces between the ribs allow you to change to 3/8" flat oval reed.

11. Gradually pull the weavers tighter to bring up the sides. After weaving about 6 1/2" from the center of the bottom, the sides should be standing up.

TO WEAVE THE SIDES:

12. Weave three rounds of 3/8" flat reed.

13. Weave three rounds of 3/8" flat oval reed. This could be a contrasting color so that the decorative chains will be more noticeable.

14. Weave three rounds of 1/2" flat reed.

15. Weave three rounds of 3/8" flat oval reed. This, too, could be of a contrasting color.

16. Weave four rounds of 1/2" flat reed.

> NOTE: Taper the last few inches of the top round for a better fitting rim.

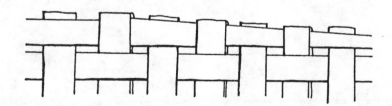

41

TO FINISH THE TOP:

17. Dampen the top of the basket and lock the spokes into place. The spokes on the outside of the top round should be cut so that they are 2" long. These spokes will be folded to the inside of the basket and tucked into the third weaver from the top as shown in the following illustration. Cut off the spokes on the inside of the basket so that they are even with the top round.

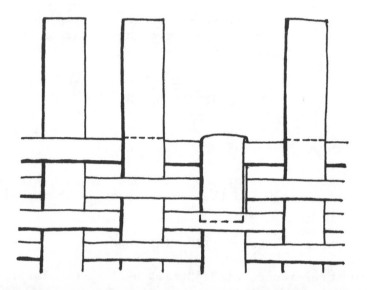

TO ATTACH THE RIM:

18. Cut two pieces of 7/8" flat oval reed 44" long for the outside and inside rims.

19. With the flat sides of the reed against the basket, place one on the inside top of the basket and one on the outside. Use clothespins to hold the rim in place.

> NOTE: Overlapping the ends of each piece on opposite sides of the basket will prevent the formation of an unsightly bulge on one side of the basket.

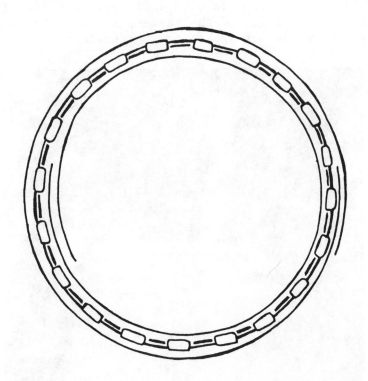

20. Using 3/16" flat oval reed, tie off the rim using any of the methods illustrated in the section entitled "Tying off Rims."

DOUBLE-BOTTOM BASKET

The double bottom is used in larger baskets. It strengthens the sides of the basket, as well as the bottom, because the number of spokes are increased.

DOUBLE-BOTTOM BASKET

Dimensions:
    Diameter of top: 16"
    Diameter of bottom: 14"
    Height: 15 1/2"

Materials:
    1/2" flat reed
    7/8" flat oval reed
    1/4" flat reed
    #2 round reed

TO MAKE THE BOTTOM:

1. Cut 16 pieces of 1/2" flat reed 50" long. Cut one piece of
    1/2" flat reed 25" long. These pieces of reed will be the
    spokes which form the framework of the basket.

2. Mark the center of the rough side of each reed with a dot 25"
    from the end.

3. Place eight spokes with the smooth side down in the following
    pattern. Use the dots to center the strips. Twine the spokes
    together with string.

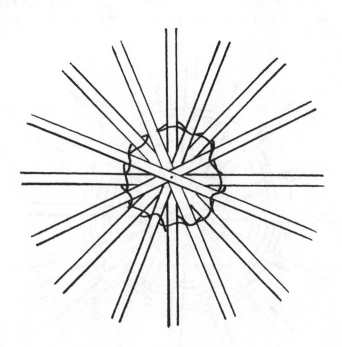

45

4. Using the dots to center the spokes, arrange the other eight spokes with smooth sides down in the following pattern. When placing the 25" spoke in the pattern, be sure to hide the end between the other spokes in the center.

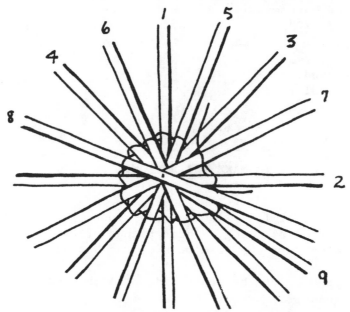

5. Twine around these spokes with string to hold them in place.

6. Soak several strands of #2 round reed in water about five minutes. Using the #2 round reed, begin weaving over one spoke, under one spoke on the uneven bottom. The beginning circle should be about 4" in diameter. Weave approximately 1 1/2". When the first weaver runs out add another reed and continue weaving.

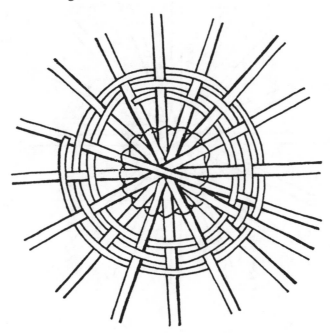

7. Place the bottom with the even spokes on top of the bottom with the uneven spokes. Arrange the spokes of the even bottom so that they will fall between the spokes of the uneven bottom. There will be one space where a spoke will be missing. This should be placed at the smallest gap so that it will be less noticable. The over one, under one weaving should have been woven to this point on the uneven set of spokes. If it is not, go back and weave to this point. As you continue to weave over one spoke, under one spoke, you will tie the two bottoms together. Weave until the diameter of the bottom is 14".

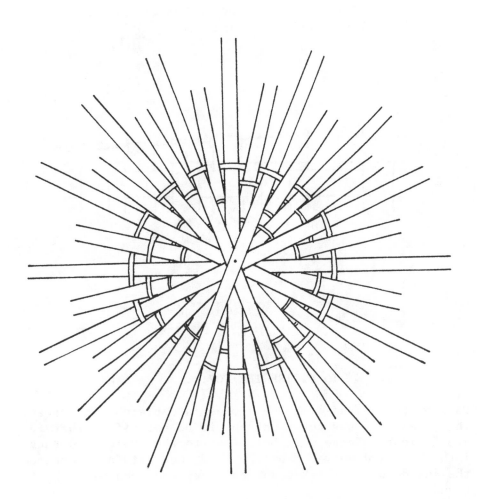

TO WEAVE THE SIDES:

8. Bend the spokes up to form the sides of the basket. The bottom should be flat.

> NOTE: Before changing the weaver to 1/2" flat reed, taper the end on one side for several inches so that the 1/2" weaver will fit into the round reed and will not leave a gap.

9. With the smooth side of the weaver turned out, continue weaving over one spoke, under one spoke using 1/2" flat reed until the height of the basket is 15".

> NOTE: Taper the last few inches of the top round for a better fitting rim.

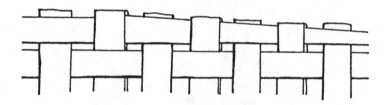

TO FINISH THE TOP:

10. Dampen the top and lock the spokes into place. The spokes on the outside of the top round should be cut off so that they are 2" long. These will be folded to the inside and tucked into the third weaver from the top. Cut off the spokes on the inside of the basket so that they are even with the top round.

TO ATTACH THE RIM:

11. Cut two pieces of 7/8" flat oval reed 55" long. With the flat sides against the basket, place one on the inside top and one on the outside top of the basket. Use clothespins to hold the rim in place.

> NOTE: When attaching two pieces of reed to form a rim, overlapping the ends on opposite sides of the basket will prevent the formation of an unsightly bulge on one side.

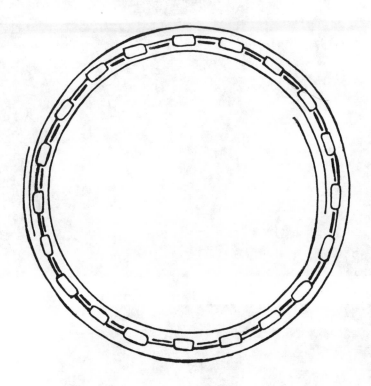

12. Using 1/4" flat reed, tie the rims to the basket. Several methods for this step are illustrated in the section entitled "Tying off Rims".

> NOTE: If the 7/8" flat oval reed begins splitting, go ahead and cut it with a knife. It will fall back into place.

Plaited Baskets

HELPFUL SUGGESTIONS FOR PLAITED BASKETS

1. The bundles of reeds are referred to as hanks. Once a hank of reed is broken, it becomes difficult to handle. Because it is impractical to retie the hanks each time a few reeds are needed, a good method of storage is necessary. Plastic trash bags and old pillow cases are ideal for this purpose.

2. One side of a flat reed is smoother than the other. To find the smooth side, dampen the reed and bend it back and forth in your hands. When bent, the rough side has a splintered appearance. In order that the basket may be as neat as possible, always turn the reed so that the smooth side will be on the outside of the basket.

   > NOTE: If the inside of the basket will be more obvious, turn the smooth side of the reed to the inside.

3. Care should be taken when wetting the flat reeds. Too much water will cause the reed to fray and split. When a direction calls for "dampening", immerse the reed in water briefly, but do not allow it to soak. Excess water may be blotted from the reed with a towel.

4. Any reeds which have been dampened, but not used, should be allowed to dry before being stored to prevent the growth of mildew.

5. Weave by bending the weavers around the stakes and placing them as close to the previous round as possible. Do not allow the weavers to bend the stakes.

6. Clothespins are handy for securing reeds in place when making baskets. (Examples: attaching the rim, splicing new weavers, and holding the top round in place on large baskets.)

7. The bottom of an unlevel basket may be flattened by doing the following:

   A. Wet the bottom of the basket.
   B. Turn it upside down on a smooth surface.
   C. Place a heavy, flat object, such as an iron skillet on the basket until the reed has dried.

8. If a stake should break, insert an icepick through the weavers and slip in a new piece of flat reed, overlapping the original stake as much as possible.

9. Upon completing the bottom of the basket, cord may be twined around the outside edges to hold the shape while turning up the sides. This may be removed after the basket is complete.

10. Weaving should be as close as possible on the sides of plaited baskets. Sometimes it is necessary to weave several rounds before the weavers will stay in place. Packing the weavers tightly together will be easier if they are wet.

11. To add a handle, the basket must have uneven ribs on the sides where the handles are to be attached.

GATHERING BASKET
(OPEN BOTTOM)

A basket of this size was used for harvesting small amounts of vegetables. The open bottom made it ideal for rinsing the produce.

GATHERING BASKET
(Open Bottom)

Dimensions:
    Diameter of top: 9"
    Diameter of bottom: 7"
    Height: 4 3/4"

Materials:
    Cane
    1/2" flat reed

TO MAKE THE BOTTOM:

1. Cut 14 pieces of 1/2" flat reed 20" long. These are called
    stakes and will be the bottom and sides of the basket (seven
    stakes in each direction).

2. Start the bottom of the basket by placing two stakes,
    vertically, side by side. Leave 1/2" between them.

3. Place one stake, horizontally, across the first two stakes and
    weave over one and under one.

4. Add a second horizontal stake which is woven opposite from the
    first one.

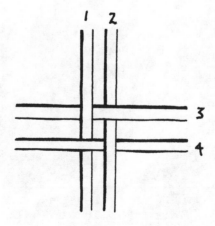

5. Continue adding stakes, counter-clockwise, until there are seven stakes in each direction

6. Adjust the stakes so that all are centered with 1/2" between each one.

7. Using string, twine around the bottom of the basket to hold the stakes in place.

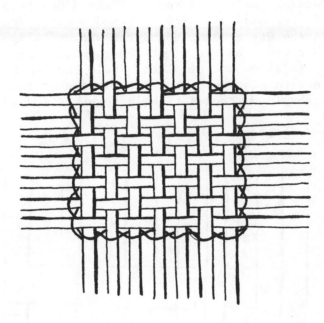

8. Wet the bottom of the basket and bend the stakes up to form the sides.

TO WEAVE THE SIDES:

NOTE: The bottom of the basket will be square. As you weave the rounds up the sides, the basket will become circular.

NOTE: The weaving will be done from the outside of the basket.

9. Cut 8 pieces of 1/2" flat reed 33" long. These are the weavers.

10. Begin weaving the bottom round of the sides by placing the weaver in the middle of any side and weaving under one, over one, all the way around. (Bend the weavers slightly as you turn the corners on the first few rounds. The first two rounds will try to slide out of place. Hold them as securely as possible with clothes pins. After three or four rounds the weavers should be packed tightly together and will then stay in place.)

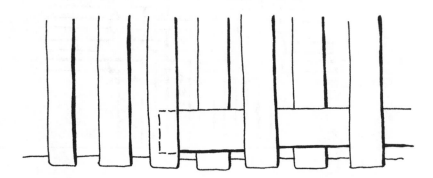

When the weaver has been inserted all the way around the basket, overlap and hide the ends.

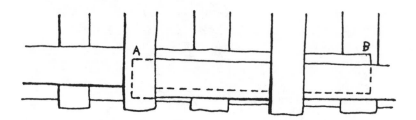

A. Weaver begins
B. Weaver overlapped and hidden

56

NOTE: Because we have allowed a few
extra inches to make the weaver more
workable, it may be necessary to cut off
some of the excess length. This will be
done after you have determined where to
hide the end.

11.   Begin weaving the second round on the side which is opposite
      where you started the first round.

          NOTE: Changing the starting point of
          each round prevents the formation of an
          unsightly bulge on one side of the
          basket.

      Weave under the stakes you wove over and over the stakes you
      wove under. Overlap and hide the ends as you did for the
      first round. Secure the weaver with clothespins.

12.   To begin the third round, start on a third side of the basket
      where no ends have been overlapped and weave exactly as you
      did in round one.

13.   At this point, stop and pack the weavers tightly together.
      Repeat this step after each round.

14.   Round four is started on the side opposite round three and
      woven exactly as you did round two.

15.   Repeat the steps for the first four rounds.

16.   For the final round, cut a piece of 1/2" flat reed 33" long.
      Trim this reed to 3/8" by cutting it lengthwise. This
      insures a neater appearance when the rim is attached. Weave
      the final round as you did round one.

17.   Pack all of the weavers tightly together.

TO FINISH THE TOP:

18. Cut off each stake on the inside of the basket so that they are even with the top weaver.

19. Dampen the basket and cut the remaining outside stakes to a length of 2". Fold these to the inside and tuck the ends into the third weaver from the top.

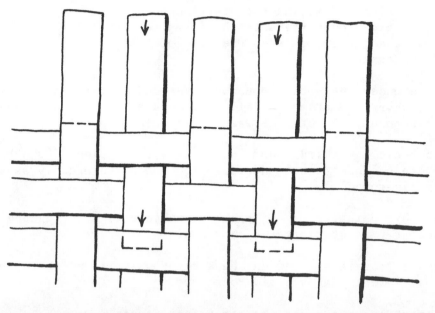

TO ATTACH THE HANDLES:

20. Cut two pieces of 1/2" flat reed 8" long.

21. The handles will be placed on opposite sides of the basket. Determine which sides you wish to use. At this point, find the two stakes on either side of the center stake (for each side) and mark them with "X's".

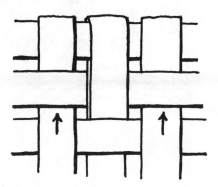

22. Wet the 8" reeds and shape them each into a "U". Bend the ends up 1".

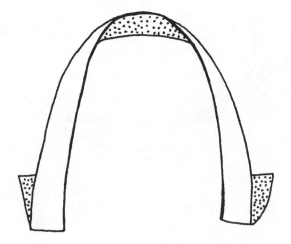

23. Place the handles at the points on each side of the basket which you have marked with "X's". Insert the ends under the second round from the top of the basket.

24. Bend the handles up so that they extend above the top of the basket. Use clothespins to hold them in place.

    NOTE: Inserting the ends at these points will insure that they are not visable from the outside of the baskets.

59

TO ATTACH THE RIM:

25. Cut two pieces of 1/2" flat reed 33" long. Place one around the inside top of the basket and one around the outside to form a rim as shown in the illustration.

> NOTE: Overlapping the ends of each piece on opposite sides of the basket will prevent the formation of an unsightly bulge on one side of the basket.

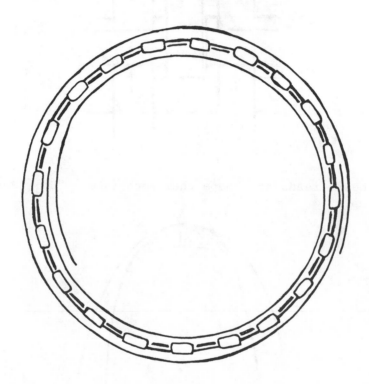

26. Using cane, tie off the rim using any of the patterns shown in the section entitled "Tying Off Rims".

BERRY BASKET

The Berry Basket is used for harvesting various fruits. The handles are close together so that a belt can be inserted through the loops attaching the basket to the waist. In similar fashion, a long shoulder strap could be used. Either method leaves one's hands free for picking berries.

BERRY BASKET

Dimensions:
    Diameter of top: 10"
    Diameter of bottom: 7"
    Height: 7"

Materials:
    1/2" flat reed
    1/4" flat reed
    7/8" flat oval read

TO MAKE THE BOTTOM:

1. Cut 14 pieces of 1/2" flat reed 26" long.

2. Cut 14 pieces of 1/4" flat reed 26" long.

> NOTE: These pieces of flat reed will be
> the stakes which form the framework of
> the basket.

3. Start the bottom by placing a piece of 1/2" flat reed and a
   piece of 1/4" flat reed vertically, side by side. Leave 1/2"
   between them.

4. Place a 1/2" stake, horizontally, across the original stakes
   and weave over one and under one.

5. Place a 1/4" stake parallel to the 1/2" stake you have just
   inserted and weave it in as shown in the illustration.

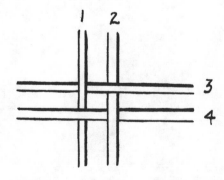

6. Continue adding stakes, counter-clockwise, around these four stakes, alternating the 1/2" and 1/4" flat reeds until there are 15 stakes, vertically, and 13 stakes, horizontally.

> NOTE: The outside, vertical stakes should be 1/4" flat reed. The outside horizontal stakes should be 1/2" flat reed.

7 Adjust the stakes so that all are centered with 1/4" between each one.

8. Twine around the bottom with string as shown in the illustration.

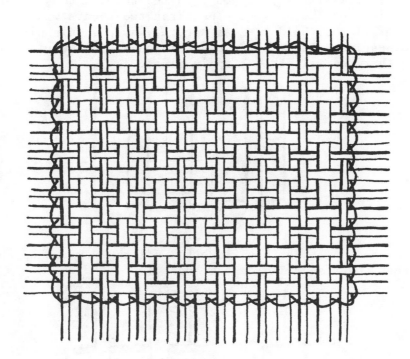

9. Wet the bottom of the basket and bend the stakes up to form the sides.

TO WEAVE THE SIDES:

NOTE: The bottom of the basket will be square. As you weave the rounds up the sides, the basket will become circular.

NOTE: The weaving will be done from the outside of the basket.

10. Cut eight pieces of 1/2" flat reed 33" long. These are the weavers.

11. To start the sides of the basket, begin weaving the bottom round of the side by placing the weaver in the middle of any side and weaving over the 1/2" stakes and under the 1/4" stakes. (Bend the weavers slightly as you turn the corners to start rounding the sides of the basket. The first two rounds will try to slide out of place. Hold them as securely as possible with clothespins. After three or four rounds the weavers will pack together and will then stay in place.

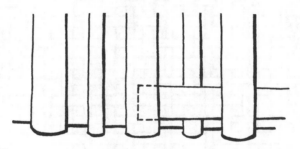

When the weaver has been inserted all the way around the basket, overlap and hide the ends.

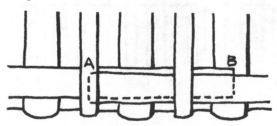

    A. Weaver begins
    B. Weaver overlapped and hidden

NOTE: Because we have allowed a few extra inches to make the weaver more workable, it may be necessary to cut off some of the excess length. This will be done after you have determined where to hide the end.

12. Begin weaving the second round on the side which is opposite where you started the first round.

> NOTE: Changing the starting point of each round prevents the formation of an unsightly bulge on one side of the basket.

Weave under the stakes you wove over and over the stakes you wove under. Overlap and hide the ends as you did for the first round. Secure the weaver with clothespins.

13. To begin the third round, start on a third side of the basket where no ends have been overlapped and weave exactly as you did in round one.

14. At this point, stop and pack the weavers together leaving 1/4" inch between them. Repeat this step after each round.

15. Round four is started on the side opposite round three and woven exactly as round two.

16. Repeat the steps for the first four rounds to complete the sides of the basket. The top of the basket should end with the 1/4" stakes on the inside of the top weaver.

TO FINISH THE TOP:

17. Cut off all 1/4" stakes (which should be on the inside of the top weaver) so that they are even with the top of the basket.

18. Cut off the 1/2" stakes to a length of 2".

19. Wet the top of the basket. Fold the stakes to the inside of the basket and tuck them into the third weaver from the top.

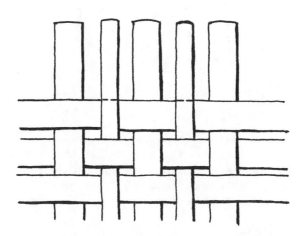

TO ATTACH THE HANDLES:

20. Cut two pieces of 1/2" flat reed 13" long.

21. The handles will be attached side-by-side on the back of the basket. The back side of the basket may be either of the two sides with fifteen stakes.

22. Determine whch side of the basket you wish to use. Find the center stake which should be a 1/2" flat reed. Use the first and third 1/2" stakes on either side of the center stake to insert the handles.

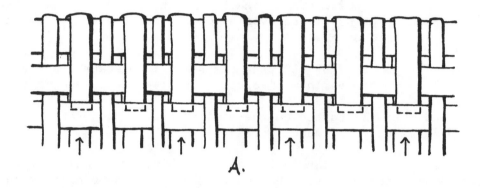

A.

A. Center Stake

23. Wet one of the 1/2" strips you cut for the handle and shape it into a "U". Bend the ends back about 2".

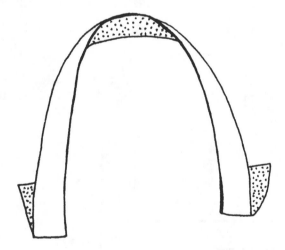

24. Tuck the ends of the handle under the third weaver (on the inside of the basket) of the designated stakes. Bend the handle up so it extends above the top of the basket and hold it in place with clothespins.

25. Repeat steps 23 - 24 for the second handle.

TO ATTACH THE RIM:

26. Cut two pieces of 7/8" flat oval reed 36" long. With the flat sides against the basket, place one on the inside top and one on the outside top of the basket. Use clothespins to hold the rim in place.

> NOTE: Overlapping the ends of each piece on opposite sides of the basket will prevent the formation of an unsightly bulge on one side of the basket.

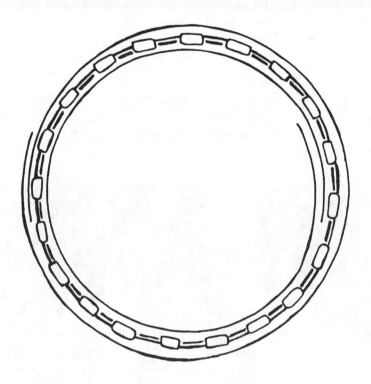

27. Using 1/4" flat reed, tie off the rim using any of the methods illustrated in the section entitled "Tying off Rims."

SHAKER WASH BASKET

The Shaker Wash Basket is an example of open weave plaiting. These baskets were used for carrying laundry because the open bottom allowed for the drainage of excess water.

Because the original baskets were made with splits from hardwood, such as oak, they were much larger. The basket shown is made from commercial reed and may be used for a variety of purposes.

SHAKER WASH BASKET

Dimensions:
    Diameter of top: 15"
    Diameter of bottom: 12"
    Height: 4"

Materials:
    7/8" flat reed
    5/8" flat reed
    1/2" flat reed
    3/8" flat reed
    1/4" flat reed
    7/8" flat oval reed

TO MAKE THE BOTTOM:

1. Cut 22 pieces of 1/2" flat reed 27" long. These pieces of reed will be the stakes which form the framework of the basket.

2. Start the bottom of the basket by placing two stakes, vertically, side by side. Leave 1/2" between them.

3. Place one stake, horizontally, across the first two stakes and weave over one and under one.

4. Add a second horizontal stake which is woven opposite from the first one.

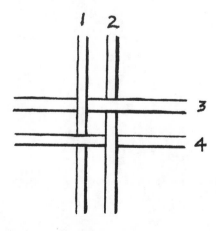

5. Continue adding stakes, counter-clockwise, until there are eleven stakes in each direction.

6. Adjust the stakes so that all are centered with 1/2" between each one.

7. Using string, twine around the bottom of the basket to hold the stakes in place.

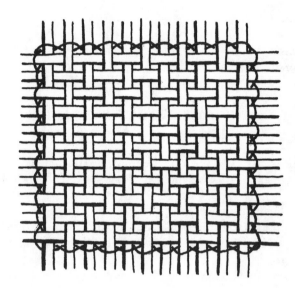

8. Wet the bottom of the basket and bend the stakes up to form the sides.

TO WEAVE THE SIDES:

NOTE: The bottom of the basket will be square. As you weave the rounds up the sides, the basket will become circular.

NOTE: The weaving will be done from the outside of the basket.

9. Cut a piece of 7/8" flat reed 53" long.

10. Begin weaving the bottom round of the sides by placing the weaver in the middle of any side and weaving under one, over one, all the way around. (Bend the weavers slightly as you turn the corners on the first few rounds. The first two rounds will try to slide out of place. Hold them as securely as possible with clothes pins. After three or four rounds the weavers will be packed tightly together and will then stay in place.)

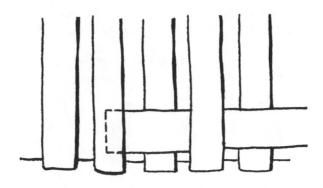

When the weaver has been inserted all the way around the basket, overlap and hide the ends.

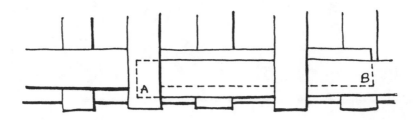

A. Weaver begins
B. Weaver overlapped and hidden

71

NOTE: Because we have allowed a few extra inches to make the weaver more workable, it may be necessary to cut off some of the excess length. This will be done after you have determined where to hide the end.

11. Cut a piece of 5/8" flat reed 53" long. Begin weaving the second round on the side which is opposite where you started the first round.

NOTE: Changing the starting point of each round prevents the formation of an unsightly bulge on one side of the basket.

Weave under the stakes you wove over and over the stakes you wove under. Overlap and hide the ends as you did for the first round. Secure the weaver with clothespins.

12. Cut a piece of 1/2" flat reed 53" long. To begin the third round, start on a third side of the basket where no ends have been overlapped and weave exactly as you did in round one.

13. At this point, stop and pack the weavers tightly together. Repeat this step after each round.

14. Cut a piece of 3/8" flat reed 53" long. Round four is started on the side opposite round three and woven exactly as you did round two.

15. For round five, cut a piece of 1/4" flat reed 53" long and weave it into the basket exactly as you did round one.

16. For the final round, cut a piece of 1/2" flat reed 53" long and weave it exactly as you did round three. The rim will be attached to this weaver.

17. Pack all of the weavers tightly together.

TO FINISH THE TOP:

18. Cut off each stake on the inside of the top round even with the top of the basket.

19. Dampen the basket and cut the remaining outside stakes to a length of 1 1/2". Fold these to the inside and tuck the ends into the third weaver from the top.

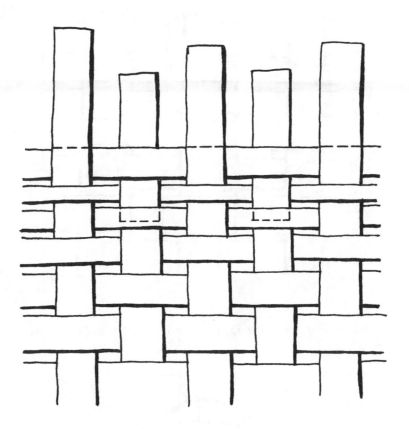

TO ATTACH THE HANDLES:

20. Cut two pieces of 7/8" flat reed 9" long.

21. The handles will be placed on opposite sides of the basket. They will be inserted on the inside. Determine which sides you wish to use. At this point, find the two stakes on either side of the center stakes (for each side) and mark them with "X's".

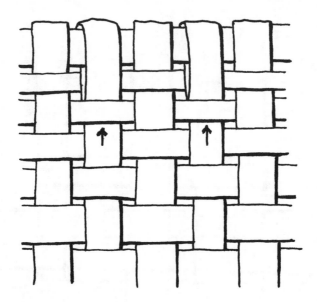

22. Wet the 9" reeds and shape them each into a "U". Bend the ends up 1".

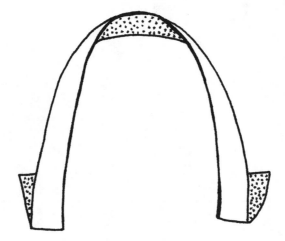

23. Place the handles at the points on each side of the basket which you have marked with "X's". Insert the ends under the third round from the top of the basket.

24. Bend the handles up so that they extend above the top of the basket. Use clothespins to hold them in place.

> NOTE: Inserting the ends at these points will insure that they are not visable from the outside of the baskets.

TO ATTACH THE RIM:

25. Cut a piece of 7/8" flat oval reed 55" long to be used on the outside top of the basket and a piece 52" long to be used on the inside. Dampen the reeds and shape them around the top of the basket in the order given above. Overlap the ends of each piece and secure them with clothespins.

> NOTE: Overlapping the ends of each piece on opposite sides of the basket will prevent the formation of an unsightly bulge on one side of the basket.

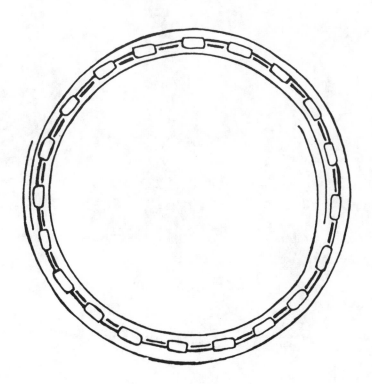

26. Tie off the rim using 1/4" flat reed. Use any method described in the section entitled "Tying Off Rims".

GATHERING BASKET
(HERRINGBONE PATTERN)

The size and construction of this basket makes it ideal for many uses. Because it has a solid bottom, this basket may be more useful than the open-bottomed variation.

GATHERING BASKET
(HERRINGBONE PATTERN)

Dimensions:
    Diameter of top: 9"
    Diameter of bottom: 8"
    Height: 4 1/2"

Materials:
    1/2" flat reed
    5/8" flat oval reed
    Cane
    "U" Shaped handle

TO MAKE THE BOTTOM:

1. Cut 26 pieces of 1/2" flat reed 23 1/2" long.

2. Place 13 pieces of reed side by side. The other 13 pieces will be woven into these to form the framework of the basket. These reeds are called stakes.

3. Start by weaving the first stake over two, under two all the way across.

4. Weave the second stake over one, under two. Continue weaving this stake over two and under two all the way across.

5. Weave the third stake under two, over two, all the way across.

6. Weave the fourth stake under one, over two. Continue weaving this stake over two and under two all the way across.

7. Repeat these four steps in sequence until all 13 stakes have been woven into the basket.

8. Make sure the stakes are even by measuring 11 1/2" to the
   centers of the seventh horizontal and vertical stakes. Mark
   each one with a dot. Adjust the stakes so that the dots
   overlap.

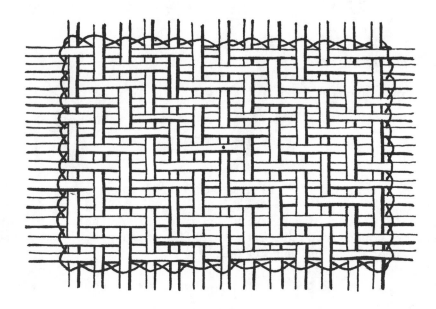

9. This illustration shows spaces between the stakes so that
   the pattern can be easily understood. Upon completing the
   bottom, pack the stakes tightly together.

10. Using string, twine around the bottom of the basket to hold
    the stakes in place. This may be removed after the basket
    is completed.

11. Dampen the bottom and bend the stakes up to form the sides.

TO WEAVE THE SIDES:

NOTE: This basket has a square bottom.
As you weave the rounds up the sides, the
basket will become circular.

12. Cut 9 pieces of 1/2" flat reed 33" long. These are the weavers.

13. Begin weaving the bottom round of the sides by placing a weaver
in the middle of one side of the basket. The pattern for the
sides will be under two, over two all the way around. Bend the
weaver slightly as you turn the corners of the first two rounds.
This will help shape the basket from a square bottom to a round
top. When the weaver has been inserted all the way around the
basket, overlap the ends several inches so that they may be
hidden behind the stakes.

NOTE: Because we have allowed a few extra
inches on each weaver, it may be necessary
to cut off some of the excess length. This
will be done after you have determined where
to hide the end.

NOTE: Clothes pins will be needed to hold
the first two weavers securely in place. After
three or four rounds these weavers may be packed
down tightly and will then stay in place.

14. Begin weaving the second round on the side which is opposite from
where you started the first round.

NOTE: Changing the starting point on each
round prevents the formation of an unsightly
bulge on one side of the basket.

To make the herringbone pattern you must advance one stake to the
right on each row, then weave over two, under two as shown in the
illustration.

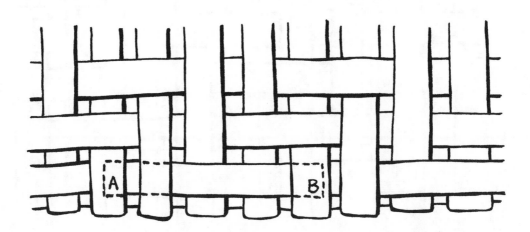

A. Weaver starts
B. End of weaver overlapped and hidden

79

15. To begin the third round, start on a third side where the ends of a weaver have not been overlapped. Advance one stake to the right and weave over two, under two. Overlap and hide the end.

16. At this point stop and pack the weavers tightly together. This packing will be necessary after each round.

17. Begin round four on the side opposite from where you started round three. Advance one stake to the right and weave over two, under two. Overlap and hide the end.

18. Repeat the steps for the first four rounds.

19. For the final round, cut a piece of 1/2" flat reed 33" long. Trim this reed to 3/8" by cutting it lengthwise. This insures a neater appearance when the rim is attached.

20. Weave the final round exactly as you did round one.

TO FINISH THE TOP:

21. Dampen the top. Lock the weavers into place by folding one stake from each outside pair to the inside and tucking it behind a weaver. Cut the remaining stakes off so that they are even with the top of the basket.

TO ATTACH THE HANDLE:

22. Using a piece of green oak 24" long, 2/3" wide and 3/16" thick shape a "U" to fit inside the basket. The ends of the "U" should be tied with a string which will hold the shape of the handle. Allow the handle to dry for 24 hours.

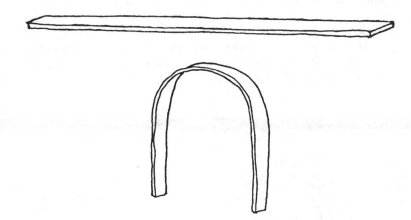

23. Using a sharp knife, taper and notch the ends of the handle so that it will slip between the center stakes and weavers on each side of the basket.

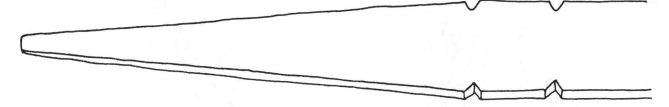

24. Position the notches above and below the top weaver and tie the handle securely to the basket using strong cord or fine wire as shown in the illustration.

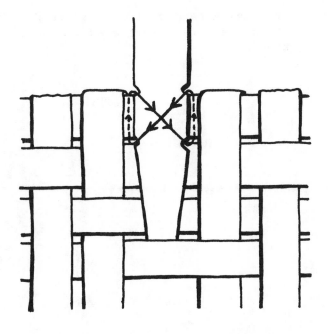

81

TO ATTACH THE RIM:

25. Cut two pieces of 1/2" flat oval reed 33" long. With the flat sides against the basket, place one on the inside top and one on the outside top of the basket. Use clothespins to hold the rim in place.

> NOTE: When attaching two pieces of reed to form a rim, overlapping the ends on opposite sides of the basket will prevent the formation of an unsightly bulge on one side.

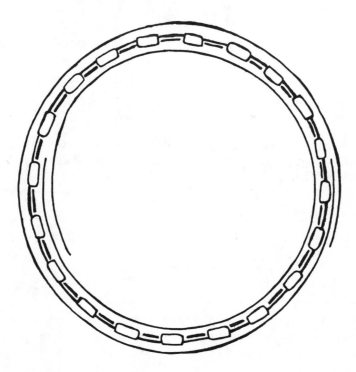

26. Tie off the rim using cane or 1/4" flat reed. Several methods for this step are illustrated in the section entitled "Tying off Rims".

MARKET BASKET

This rectangular basket with a center handle was used originally for carrying produce long distances to the market. It can be used for a variety of practical purposes.

MARKET BASKET

Dimensions:
   Diameter of top: 9" x 18"
   Diameter of bottom: 6 1/2"
   Height: 7" (without handle)

Materials:
   1/2" flat reed
   5/8" flat oval reed
   Cane or 1/4" flat reed

TO MAKE THE BOTTOM:

1. Cut 21 pieces of 1/2" flat reed 26" long.

2. Cut 13 pieces of 1/2" flat reed 36" long.

> NOTE: These pieces of reed will be
> the stakes which form the framework
> of the basket.

3. Place the 21 pieces of 26" stakes vertically, side by side.
   Leave 1/4" between each one.

4. Weave each 36" stake over one, under one through the vertical
   stakes until all 13 are in place.

> NOTE: The illustration shows spaces
> between the stakes so that the
> pattern can be easily illustrated.

5. Upon completing the bottom, pack the 36" stakes as closely
   together was possible leaving 1/4" between the 26" stakes.

> NOTE: Variations in packing will
> create a different shaped bottom.

Center the stakes so that they are as even as possible around
the outside edges.

84

6. Using string, twine around the bottom of the basket to hold the stakes in place.

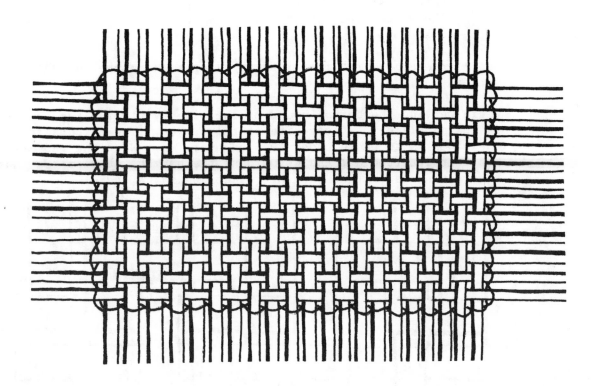

7. Dampen the bottom of the basket and bend the stakes up to form the sides.

85

TO WEAVE THE SIDES:

> NOTE: This basket has a rectangular
> bottom. As you weave the rounds up
> the sides, the basket will form an
> oval top.

8. Cut 12 pieces of 1/2" flat reed 50" long. These are the
    weavers.

9. Begin weaving the bottom round of the side by placing the weaver
    in the middle of one long side of the basket. The pattern for
    the sides is to weave under two and over two. When the weaver
    has been inserted all the way around the basket, overlap the ends
    several inches so that they are hidden behind a stake.

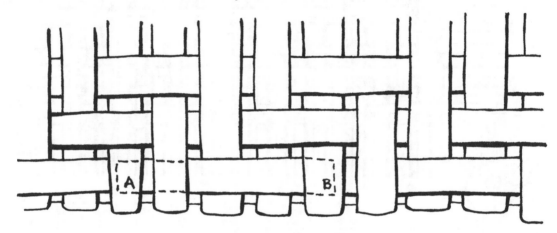

A. Weaver starts
B. End of weaver overlapped and hidden

10. Begin weaving the second round on the side which is opposite from
    where you started the first round.

> NOTE: Changing the starting point on
> each round prevents the formation of
> an unsightly bulge on one side of the
> basket.

To make the herringbone pattern you must advance one stake to the
right on each row, then weave over two, under two.

11. To begin the third round, start on a third side where the ends of
    a weaver have not been overlapped and, advancing one stake to the
    right, weave over two, under two. Overlap and hide the ends
    behind the stakes.

12. At this point stop and pack the weavers tightly together. This packing will be necessary after each round.

13. Begin round four on the side opposite from where you started round three and, advancing one stake to the right, weave over two, under two. Overlap and hide the ends.

14. Continue adding the weavers, repeating the first four rounds, until all 12 rounds are in place.

15. Pack each round tightly into place.

TO FINISH THE TOP:

16. Dampen the top of the basket and lock the stakes into place by folding one stake from each outside pair to the inside and tucking it behind a weaver. Cut off the remaining stakes so that they are even with the top.

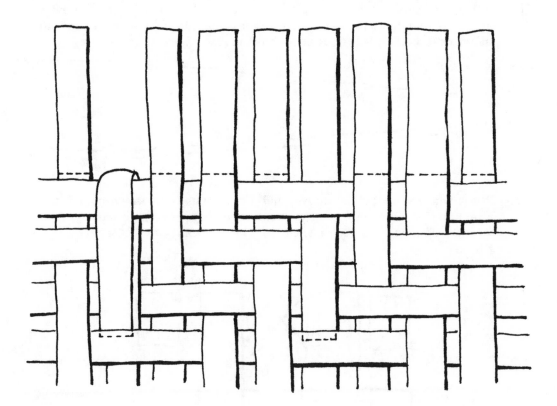

TO ATTACH THE HANDLE:

17. Using a piece of green oak 24" long, 2/3" wide and 3/16" thick shape a "U" to fit inside the basket, which is approximately 9" in diameter. The ends of the "U" should be tied with a string which will hold the shape of the handle. Allow the handle to dry for 24 hours.

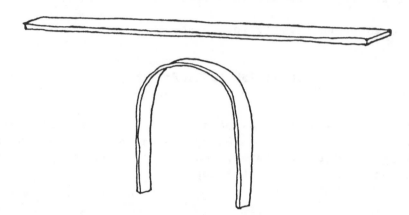

18. Using a sharp knife, taper and notch the ends of the handle so that the handle will slide between the center stakes and weavers on each side of the basket.

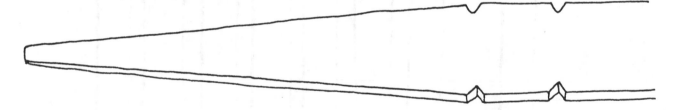

19. Position the notches above and below the top weaver and tie the handle securely to the basket using strong cord or fine wire. Repeat the "X" shown in the illustration several times.

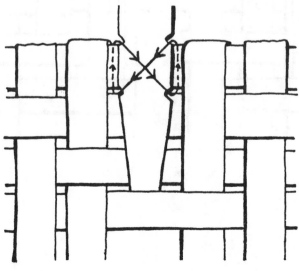

TO ATTACH THE RIM:

20. Cut two pieces of 7/8" flat oval reed 53" long for the outside and inside rims.

21. With the flat sides of the reed against the basket, place one on the inside top of the basket and one on the outside. Use clothespins to hold the rim in place.

> NOTE: Overlapping the ends of each piece on opposite sides of the basket will prevent the formation of an unsightly bulge on one side of the basket.

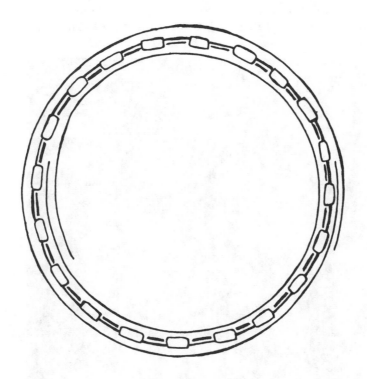

22. Using 1/4" flat oval reed or cane, tie off the rim using any of the methods illustrated in the section entitled "Tying off Rims."

BURDEN BASKET

The original basket was made of oak splits, some of which had been dyed. It is owned by Bill and Betty Sambleson and is an original North Carolina Indian basket.

BURDEN BASKET

Dimensions:
    Diameter of top: 10"
    Diameter of bottom: 9" x 10"
    Height: 14"

Materials:
    5/8" flat reed
    1/2" flat reed
    3/8" flat reed
    1/4" flat reed

NOTE: Dyed materials will be used in this basket.
The following lengths of reed will need to be dyed
ahead and dried so that they will be ready to use.
Any commercial dye may be used.

10 pieces of 5/8" brown flat reed 46" long
4 pieces of 3/8" brown flat reed 45" long
1 piece of 1/4" brown flat reed 95" long
10 pieces of 1/4" brown flat reed 45" long
4 pieces of 1/4" red flat reed 42" long
4 pieces of 3/8" red flat reed 45" long

NOTE: The directions will call for tan reed. You
may use the natural buff color of the reed or after
the basket is complete, cover the entire basket
with a light tan-colored stain. The brown and red
will still be seen.

91

TO MAKE THE BOTTOM:

1. Cut ten pieces of tan 5/8" flat reed 46" long.

2. Cut ten pieces of brown 5/8" flat reed 46" long.

3. Cut eight pieces of tan 3/8" flat reed 15" long.

> NOTE: These pieces of reed will be the stakes which form the framework of the basket. The remaining pieces of reed will be the weavers.

4. Mark the center of each strip with a dot.

5. Arrange the stakes smooth sides down parallel in the following order:

a. 5/8" tan 46" long

b. 3/8" tan 15" long

c. 5/8" brown 46" long

d. 3/8" tan 15" long

e. 5/8" tan 46" long

f. 3/8" tan 15" long

g. 5/8" brown 46" long

h. 3/8" tan 15" long

i. 5/8" tan 46" long

j. 3/8" tan 15" long

k. 5/8" brown 46" long

l. 3/8" tan 15" long

m. 5/8" tan 46" long

n. 3/8" tan 15" long

o. 5/8" brown 46" long

p. 3/8" tan 15" long

q. 5/8" tan 46" long

6. Using the dots as a guide, adjust the stakes so that the ends are even. Begin weaving by following the pattern below. Leave 1/4" to 3/8" space between the weavers only. Be sure the stakes are packed closely together.

> NOTE: If the directions say to weave under all of the brown stakes, then you would weave over all of the remaining stakes.

a. Weave a brown 5/8" stake under all brown 5/8" stakes

b. Weave a tan 5/8" stake under all tan 5/8" stakes

c. Weave a brown 5/8" stake over all tan 5/8" stakes

d. Weave a tan 5/8" stake under all tan 5/8" stakes

e. Repeat the above steps as follows: a, b, c, d, a, b, c

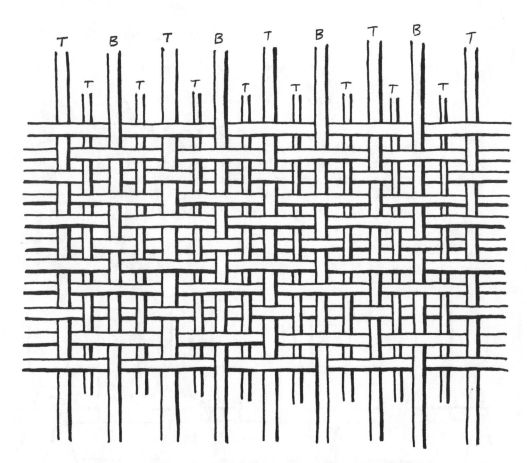

> NOTE: The illustration shows spaces between all stakes so that the pattern can be easily illustrated. The stakes marked by T (tan) and B (brown) should be packed closely together.

7. Center all of the stakes using the dots as a guide.

8. Twine around the bottom of the basket with heavy string to hold the stakes in place.

93

TO WEAVE THE SIDES:

9. Dampen the bottom of the basket and bend the stakes up to form the sides.

10. Weave the following pieces of reed around the sides overlapping and hiding the ends behind stakes. If the directions say to weave under the brown stakes, then you would weave over all of the other stakes.

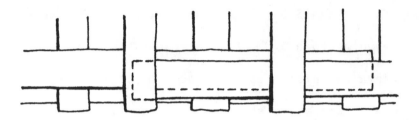

a. 3/8" tan weaver over all brown 5/8" stakes

b. 3/8" tan weaver over all tan 5/8" stakes

c. 3/8" tan weaver under all tan 5/8" stakes.

> NOTE: At this point the 15" tan 3/8" stakes should end. Take the ends and turn them toward each other forming the pattern shown in the illustration. If these ends should show above the third round, cut them off even with the third round.

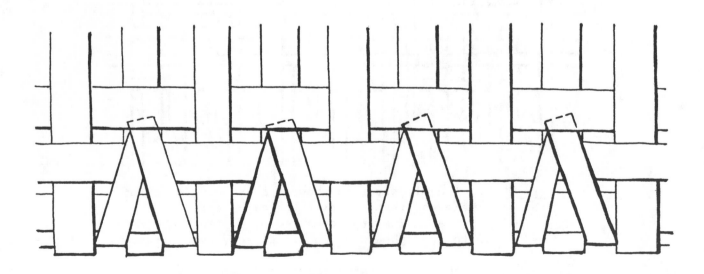

d. 1/4" brown weaver under brown 5/8" stakes

e. 3/8" red weaver under tan 5/8" stakes

f. 5/8" tan weaver under brown 5/8" stakes

g. 3/8" red weaver under tan 5/8" stakes

h. 1/4" brown weaver under brown 5/8" stakes

i. 1/2" tan weaver under tan 5/8" stakes

j. 3/8" tan weaver under brown 5/8" stakes

k. 1/4" brown weaver under tan 5/8" stakes

l. Repeat j and k four times

m. 3/8" tan weaver under brown 5/8" stakes

n. 1/2" tan weaver under tan 5/8" stakes

o. 3/8" brown weaver under brown 5/8" stakes

p. 3/8" red weaver under tan 5/8" stakes

q. 1/2" tan weaver under brown 5/8" stakes

r. 3/8" red weaver under tan 5/8" stakes

s. 3/8" brown weaver under brown 5/8" stakes

11. Begin pulling the weavers tighter to pull in the sides.

t. 3/8" tan weaver under tan 5/8" stakes

u. 1/4" tan weaver under brown 5/8" stakes

v. 1/4" red weaver under tan 5/8" stakes

w. 1/4" tan weaver under 5/8" brown stakes

12. Taper the brown stakes as shown in the illustration.

13. Continue weaving, pulling the weavers closer together, as follows:

    x. 1/4" red weaver under tan 5/8" stakes

    y. 1/4" tan weaver under tapered brown stakes

    z. 1/4" red weaver under tan 5/8" stakes

  aa. 1/4" brown weaver under tapered brown stakes

  bb. 1/4" tan weaver under tan 5/8" stakes

  cc. 1/4" brown weaver under tapered brown stakes

  dd. 1/4" red weaver under tan 3/8" stakes

  ee. 1/4" tan weaver under tapered brown stakes

  ff. 1/4" brown weaver under tan 5/8" stakes

  gg. 3/8" tan weaver under tapered brown stakes

TO FINISH THE TOP:

14. Dampen the top of the basket and lock the stakes into place. The stakes on the outside of the top round should be cut so that they are 2" long. These stakes will be folded to the inside of the basket and tucked into the third weaver from the top as shown in the following illustration. Cut off the stakes on the inside of the basket so that they will be even with the top round.

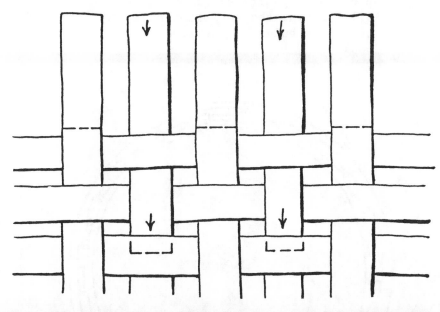

TO ATTACH THE RIM:

15. Cut two pieces of 1/2" flat oval reed 31" long for the outside and inside rims.

16. With the flat sides of the reed against the basket, place one on the inside top of the basket and one on the outside. Use clothespins to hold the rim in place.

    > NOTE: Overlapping the ends of each piece on opposite sides of the basket will prevent the formation of an unsightly bulge on one side of the basket.

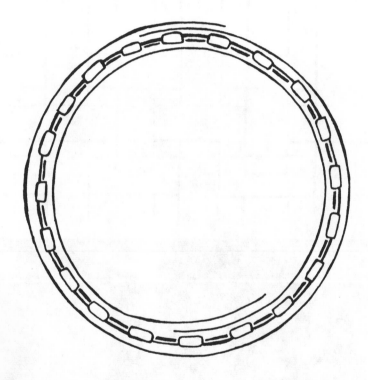

17. Using 1/4" brown flat reed, tie off the rim using any of the methods illustrated in the section entitled "Tying off Rims."

CHEESE BASKET

This hexagonal basket is an example of open-weave plaiting. Of Shaker origin, the basket was used originally in part of the cheese-making process.

CHEESE BASKET

Dimensions:
   Diameter of top: 14"
   Diameter of bottom: 12"
   Height: 4"

Materials:
   1/2" flat reed
   7/8" flat oval reed
   1/4" flat oval

TO MAKE THE BOTTOM:

1. Cut 18 pieces of 1/2" flat reed 28" long. Mark the center of
    the rough side of each strip with a dot 14" from the end.
    These pieces of reed will be the stakes which form the
    framework of the basket.

2. Place six stakes with the smooth side down parallel to each
    other and approximately 1 1/2" apart.

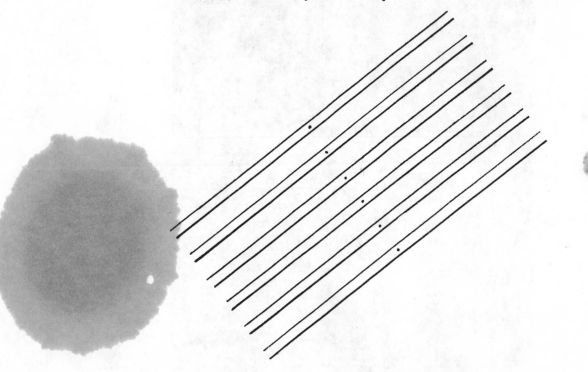

3. Place six stakes with the smooth side down parallel to each
    other on top of the first six forming an "X". The second set
    of stakes should be approximately 1 1/2" apart.

4. Line up the dots on each stake as shown in the illustration.

    NOTE: To prevent the stakes from shifting
    as you weave step 5, secure the ends by
    using masking tape or placing heavy objects
    (such as books) on top of them.

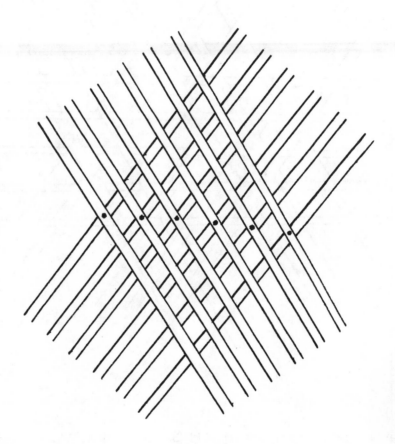

5. Weave the last six stakes with the smooth side down from
    right to left, going under the stakes in the first step
    (those on the bottom) and over the stakes in the second step
    (those on top).

6. Adjust the stakes so that they are even using the dots as
    guides. Some of the dots will be hidden.

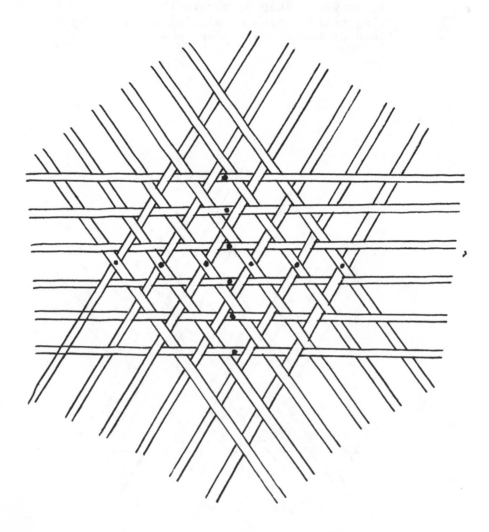

7. The bottom of the basket will be six sided. There will be
    three six-sided shapes on each outside edge. Adjust the
    stakes so that the spaces between them are equal.

8. Wet the bottom and bend the stakes up to form the sides of
    the basket.

TO WEAVE THE SIDES:

9. Lock the stakes in place by putting the stake on the right on top of the stake on the left in pairs.

10. Cut two pieces of 1/2" flat reed 44" long and dampen them. These are the weavers.

11. With the smooth side out, begin weaving one of the 44" weavers around the side by going over the stake on the outside and under the stake on the inside. This locks these stakes together and will create the six-sided pattern up the side. Overlap the end of the flat reed several inches so that it will not slip out.

12. Lock the stakes again by putting the stake on the right on top of the stake on the left in pairs.

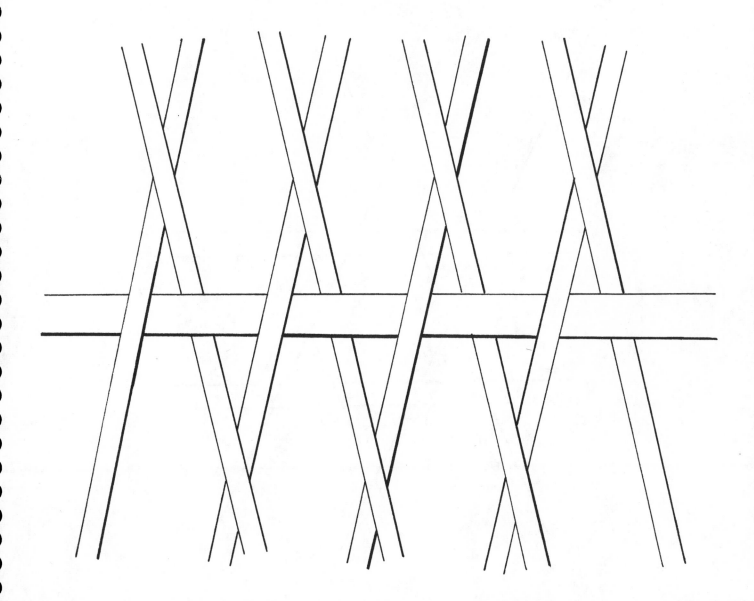

13. Begin weaving the second 44" weaver around the side by going over the stake on the outside and under the stake on the inside. Overlap the ends of the flat reed several inches.

14. Lock the stakes again by putting the stake on the right on top of the stake on the left in pairs.

TO FINISH THE TOP:

15. Dampen the top of the basket and lock the stakes into place by folding the excess length of the stakes over and tucking the ends between the stakes on the side.

   > NOTE: Fold the stakes as closely as possible to the top round of the basket so that they will be neatly covered by the rim.

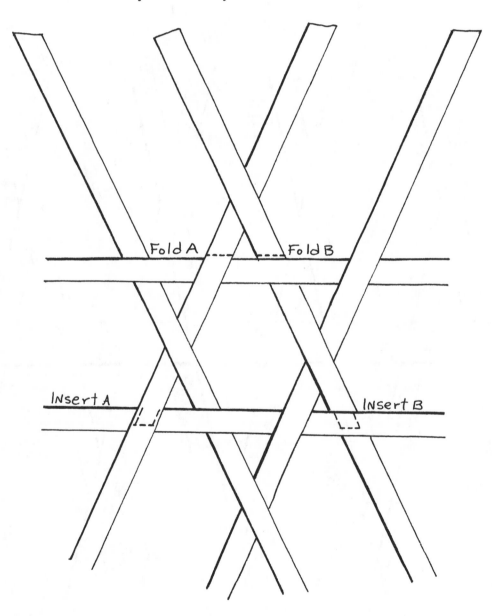

TO ATTACH THE RIM:

16. Cut two pieces of 7/8" flat oval reed 48" long for the outside and inside rims.

17. With the flat sides of the reed against the basket, place one on the inside top of the basket and one on the outside. Use clothespins to hold the rim in place.

> NOTE: Overlapping the ends of each piece on opposite sides of the basket will prevent the formation of an unsightly bulge on one side of the basket.

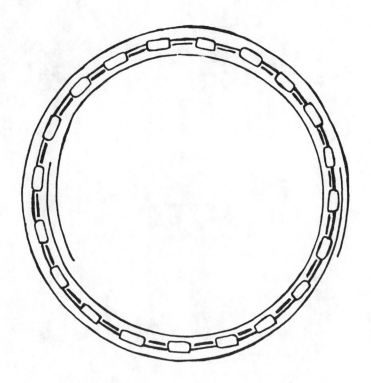

18. Using 1/4" flat oval reed, tie off the rim using any of the methods illustrated in the section entitled "Tying off Rims."

22" CHEESE BASKET

Dimensions:
    Diameter of top: 22"
    Diameter of bottom: 22"
    Height: 6"

Materials:
    1/4" flat reed
    1/2" flat reed
    7/8" flat oval reed

Wickerwork

HELPFUL SUGGESTIONS FOR WICKERWORK

1. The bundles of reeds are referred to as hanks. Once a hank of reed is broken, it becomes difficult to handle. Because it is impractical to retie the hanks each time a few reeds are needed, a good method of storage is necessary. Plastic trash bags and old pillow cases are ideal for this purpose.

2. It will be necessary to soak the round reed for several minutes to insure that it will not break. For the larger round reed, a longer soaking time will be required.

3. Any reeds which have been dampened, but not used, should be allowed to dry before being stored to prevent the growth of mildew.

4. Clothespins are handy for securing reeds in place when making baskets. (Examples: weaving the rim, splicing new weavers, and holding the top round in place on large baskets.)

5. If a spoke should break, insert an ice pick through the weavers and slip in a new piece of round reed beside of the original spoke.

6. Most baskets have a flat bottom. An inexperienced basketmaker has a tendency to force the weavers into place causing the spokes to turn up too soon. The weavers need to be bent around the spokes allowing them to remain flat on the table.

   One way to eliminate this problem is, after a few rounds, turn the basket over and weave from the other side. Alternating the weaving in this manner may help to keep the bottom flat.

7. The bottom of an unlevel basket may be flattened by doing the following:

   A. Wet the bottom of the basket.
   B. Turn it upside down on a smooth surface.
   C. Place a heavy, flat object, such as an iron skillet on the basket until the reed has dried.

NUT BASKET

Because of its simplicity, the nut basket is good for
beginning basketmakers. As the name implies, it may be used
for holding nuts, but it is also suitable for other uses.
The size may be altered by changing the lengths of the
spokes.

NUT BASKET

Dimensions:
    Diameter of bottom: 5"
    Height: 3"

Materials:
    #2 round reed
    #5 round reed

TO MAKE THE BOTTOM:

1. Soak several strands of #2 round reed in warm water for about five minutes.

2. While the #2 round reed is soaking, cut six pieces of #5 round reed 20" long. These reeds will be the spokes which form the framework of the basket.

3. Using a sharp knife, make a slot in the middle of three of the reeds. The opening should be wide enough to insert the three other spokes.

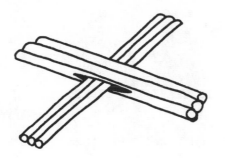

4. Using #2 round reed, twine around three spokes at a time for two rounds.

5. Dampen the spokes again and twine around each one to separate them. Continue to weave until the bottom of the basket is 5" in diameter.

TO WEAVE THE SIDES:

6. Dampen the spokes again and bend them up to form the sides of the basket.

    NOTE: The angle formed when the sides are turned up will be the basketmaker's choice. It may be a right angle making an upright side (⊔) or a more obtuse angle (◡) which will make the top of the basket wider.

7. Continue to twine around each spoke until 2" have been woven up the sides.

TO FINISH THE TOP:

8. The top is finished by turning the spokes down into the sides of the basket.

   NOTE: The spokes need to be quite wet
   to prevent them from breaking.

9. The following illustrations show two ways that the top may be finished.

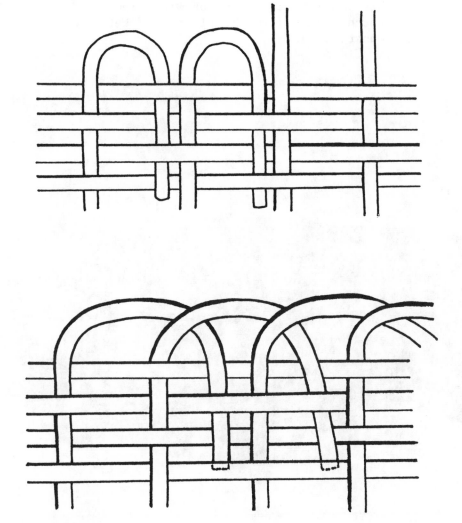

WICKER BASKET WITH BAND

This small basket combines wickering with the simple weaving technique used in the plaited baskets and can be quickly constructed.

WICKER BASKET WITH BAND

Dimensions:
    Diameter of Top: 5 1/2"
    Diameter of bottom: 5 1/2"
    Height: 4"

Materials:
    #2 round reed
    1/4" flat reed

TO MAKE THE BOTTOM:

1. Soak several strands of #2 round reed in warm water for several minutes for flexibility and to prevent breakage.

2. Cut eight pieces of #2 round reed 26" long. These pieces of reed will be the spokes which form the frame of the basket.

3. Place four spokes perpendicular to and on top of the other four spokes, making sure they are centered.

4. Using #2 round reed, twine around four spokes at a time for two rounds.

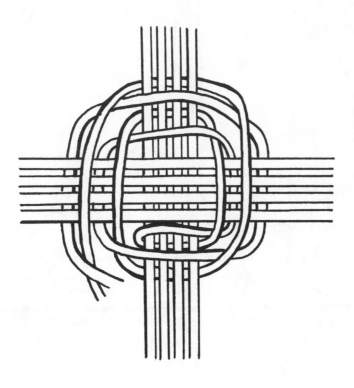

115

5. Dampen the spokes thoroughly and separate them by twining around two spokes at a time for four rounds.

6. Continue separating the spokes by twining around each one until the diameter of the bottom of the basket is 5 1/2".

TO WEAVE THE SIDES:

7. Cut 16 pieces of #2 round reed 11" long.

8. Insert one of these pieces of reed beside each of the spokes in the bottom of the basket.

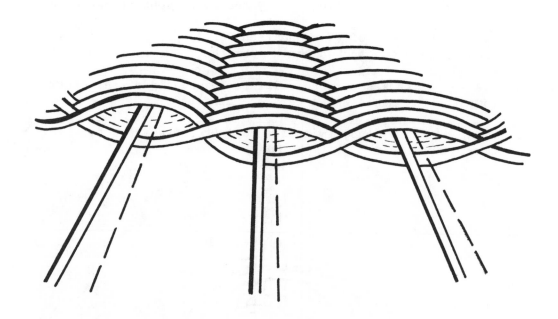

9. Dampen the spokes again to prevent breakage.

10. Twine around each spoke for four rounds.

11. To form the sides, dampen the basket and bend the spokes up.

12. Continue twining up the sides of the basket for 1"

13. Cut seven pieces of 1/4" flat reed 26" long and dampen them.

14. Using one of the 1/4" flat reeds, weave over one, under one around the basket for one round. Overlap and hide the ends as much as possible behind the spokes.

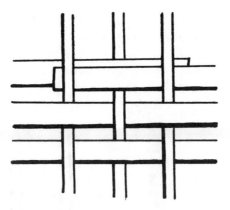

15. Continue adding the 1/4" weavers until seven rounds have been completed.

16. Using a strand of dampened #2 round reed, continue twining for 1".

TO FINISH THE TOP:

17. A four-step method will be used to finish the top. To eliminate confusion, complete each step all the way around the basket before going to the next step.

>   NOTE: Clothespins will be needed to hold the spokes in place.

18. Looking at the outside of the basket, bend the spoke on the left behind the spoke on the right and bring it to the outside of the basket.

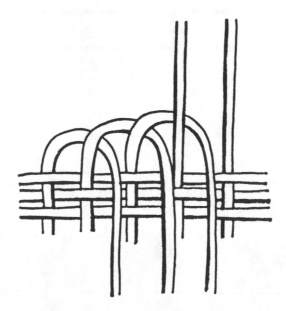

19. Bend the spoke on the left up and behind the spoke on the right.

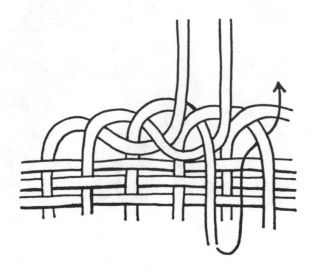

20. Place the upright spoke so that it rests against and follows the top of the curved spoke to its right. Bring the spoke to the outside of the basket.

21. Place the spoke so that it rests against and on top of the spoke forming the bottom curve and bring the spoke to the inside of the basket.

22. When all four steps have been completed, cut off the excess lengths of the reeds on the inside of the basket. Leave enough length so that the reeds will not slip out of place.

NANCY'S BASKET

This small basket with a handle is copied from an old basket owned by Nancy Scott of Smithfield, North Carolina.

NANCY'S BASKET

Dimensions:
    Diameter of top: 5"
    Diameter of bottom: 5"
    Height: 3 1/4"

Materials:
    #1 round reed
    #2 round reed
    #5 round reed

TO MAKE THE BOTTOM:

1. Cut ten pieces of #5 round reed 5" long. These will be the spokes which form the bottom of the basket.

2. Using a sharp knife, cut a slot in the middle of five of the spokes. Make sure the opening is large enough to insert the other five spokes.

3. Insert five of the spokes into each of the five spokes which have openings.

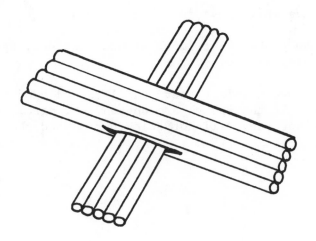

4. Soak several strands of #1 round reed in warm water for several minutes for flexibility and to avoid breakage.

5. Twine around five spokes at a time for two rounds.

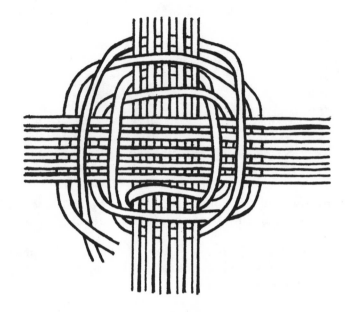

6. Wet the reeds which have just been twined.

7. Separate the spokes by twining around each one, spacing them as evenly as possible.

8. Continue to weave this pattern until the edge of the bottom is reached. If the spokes are uneven in length, cut off the excess so that they will not stick out beyond the weaving.

TO WEAVE THE SIDES:

9. Cut 41 pieces of #2 round reed 11" long.

10. Insert a #2 round reed on each side of the #5 round reed.

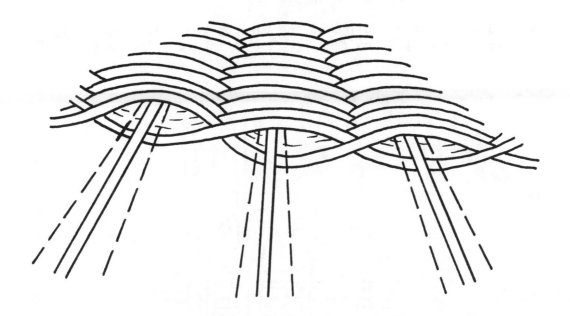

11. There will be one piece of reed left. It should be inserted in the area with the widest available space between the #2 round reed spokes.

12. Soak several strands of #1 round reed in warm water for several minutes.

13. Using the #1 round reed, twine around each spoke of #2 round reed for 1/2".

14. Using #2 round reed, weave over two, under two, up the side of the basket until 3" of weaving has been completed.

> NOTE: Because an uneven number of spokes have been used, the over, under pattern will spiral up the side of the basket.

TO FINISH THE TOP:

15. A four-step method will be used to finish the top. To eliminate confusion, complete each step all the way around the basket before going to the next step.

   NOTE: Clothespins will be needed to hold the spokes in place.

16. Looking at the outside of the basket, bend the spoke on the left behind the spoke on the right and bring it to the outside of the basket.

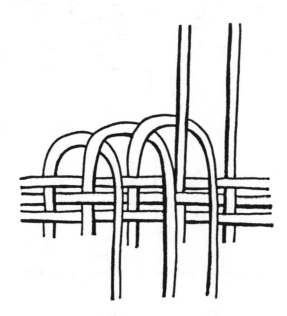

17. Bend the spoke on the left up and behind the spoke on the right.

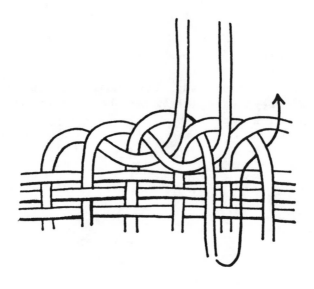

18. Place the upright spoke so that it rests against and follows the top of the curved spoke to its right. Bring the spoke to the outside of the basket.

19. Place the spoke so that it rests against and on top of the spoke forming the bottom curve and bring the spoke to the inside of the basket.

20. When all four steps have been completed, cut off the excess lengths of the reeds on the inside of the basket. Leave enough length so that the reeds will not slip out of place.

TO ATTACH THE HANDLE:

21. Cut a piece of #5 round reed 17" long.

22. Sharpen the ends with a pencil sharpener.

23. The ends of the handle will be inserted from the outside near the bottom on opposite sides of the basket.

24. Wrap the handle with #2 round reed using several strands at the same time.

25. Secure the handle by weaving the strands of #2 round reed into the sides of the basket where the handle is inserted.

26. Weave from side to side until the handle has been covered and is well secured.

PRODUCE BASKET

This basket is approximately one-half bushel in size. It is similar to baskets used in South America to gather coffee beans.

PRODUCE BASKET

Dimensions:
    Diameter of top: 17"
    Diameter of bottom: 14"
    Height: 7"

Materials:
    #6 round reed
    #3 round reed
    #2 round reed
    1/4" flat reed
    3/8" flat oval reed

TO MAKE THE BOTTOM:

1. Cut 12 pieces of #6 round reed 46" long. These reeds will be used to form the framework of the basket.

2. Arrange the spokes as shown in the illustration.

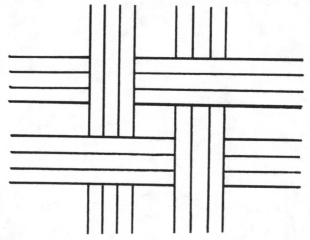

3. Dampen a piece of #2 round reed and weave over three spokes, under three spokes for four rounds. Cut the weaver off and hide the end as much as possible.

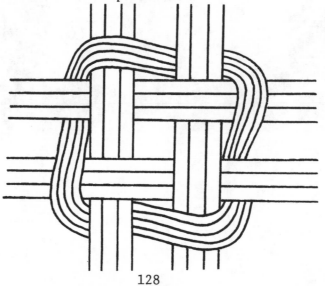

4. Soak the spokes thoroughly and bend them slightly to separate them as evenly as possible.

5. Using #3 round reed, twine around each spoke for five rounds. Cut off and hide the end of the weaver.

6. At this point, more spokes will need to be inserted. Cut seven pieces of #6 round reed 24" long.

7. Sharpen one end of each spoke and insert them into the rounds previously formed as shown in the illustration.

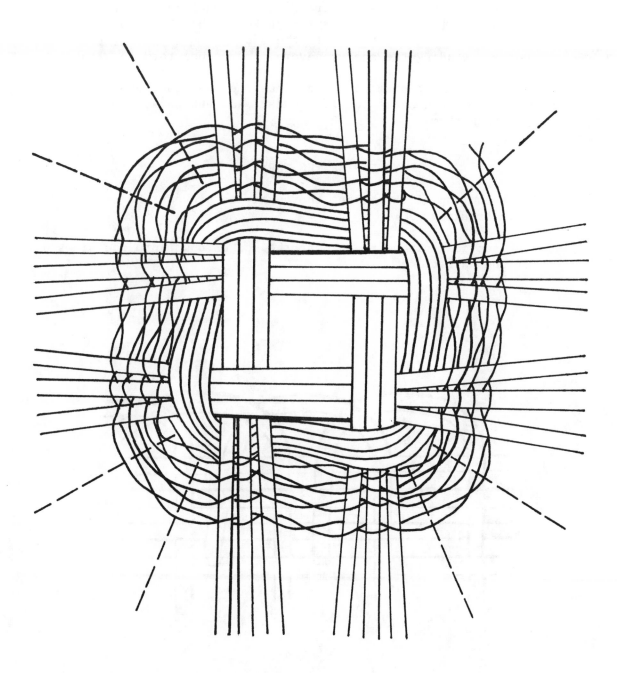

8. Using 1/4" flat reed, weave over two, under two for eleven rounds. Cut off the excess length of the weaver.

9. Using a piece of dampened #3 round reed, twine around each spoke for six rounds.

10. Wet a piece of 3/8" flat oval reed and weave over two, under two for three rounds.

TO WEAVE THE SIDES:

11. Wet the spokes to prevent breaking them when forming the sides. At this point, bend the spokes up so that the transition from the bottom to the side forms a smooth, even curve. Bending the spokes severely may cause them to break.

12. Using 3/8" flat oval reed, continue the over two, under two pattern up the sides for 18 rounds. Add new weavers by splicing them.

TO FINISH THE TOP:

13. Soak the top of the basket thoroughly to prevent the spokes from breaking.

14. The top is finished by turning the spokes down into the sides of the basket.

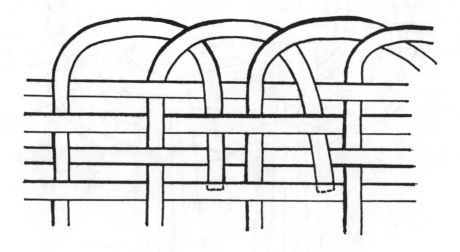

SEWING BASKET WITH LID

The sewing basket may be made with either a flat or domed lid. The construction of the basket is such that a lip is formed upon which the lid will rest.

SEWING BASKET WITH LID

Dimensions:
 Diameter of top: 13"
 Diameter of bottom: 10"
 Height without the lid: 5"
 Height of the rounded lid: 4"
 Diameter of the domed lid: 12"
 Diameter of the flat lid: 12"

Materials:
 #6 round reed
 #2 round reed

TO MAKE THE BOTTOM:

1. Cut six pieces of #6 round reed 10" long. These pieces of reed will be the spokes which form the frame of the basket.

2. Soak a few strands of the #2 round reed in warm water for five minutes.

3. Place three 10" pieces of #6 round reed on top of the other three pieces of reed as shown in the illustration.

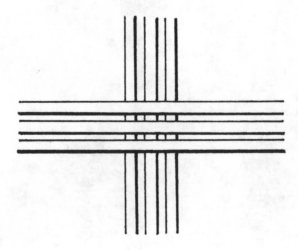

4. Using a strand of the dampened #2 round reed, twine around three spokes at a time for two rounds.

5. Dampen the spokes thoroughly and separate them as evenly as possible by bending each outside spoke.

6. Twine around each spoke until the edge is reached. This will complete the bottom.

TO WEAVE THE SIDES:

7. Cut 24 pieces of #2 round reed 20" long.

8. Place one piece of #2 round reed on each side of the original twelve spokes by inserting them into the weaving. These reeds will be the spokes used to form the sides of the basket.

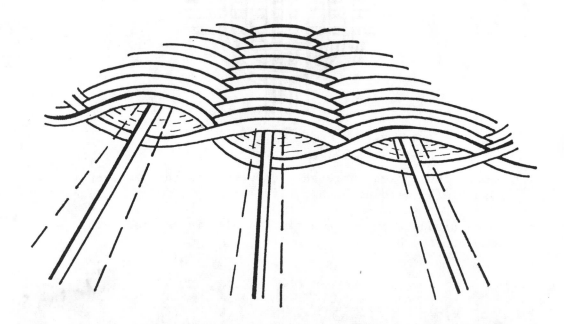

9. Dampen the bottom of the basket and bend the #2 round reed spokes up to form the sides.

10. Twine around each spoke for 2".

11. Cut 24 pieces of #2 round reed 14" long.

12. Insert one of these 14" reeds beside of each spoke by inserting it into the weaving. These reeds should be added, consistently, either to the right or left of the original spokes.

13. Twine around each of these spokes for about two inches.

TO MAKE THE LIP:

14.   Dampen all of the spokes.

15.   Bend the spokes which were added last to the inside of the basket.

> NOTE: Every other spoke will be bent to the inside of the basket. One inch below the rim of the basket, a lip will be formed upon which the lid can rest.

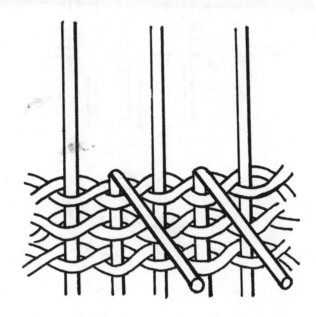

16.   Twine around the inside spokes for six rounds or about 1".

17.   To finish off the lip, a four-step method will be used. To eliminate confusion, complete each step all the way around the basket before going to the next step.

> NOTE: Clothespins will be needed to hold the spokes in place.

18. Beginning with any spoke, bend it to the right and behind the spoke on the right, bringing it to the top side of the lip. Continue this step all the way around the basket.

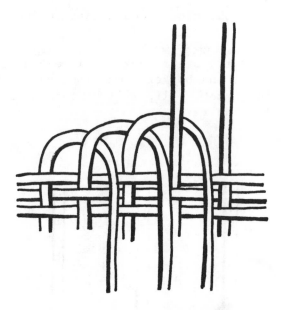

19. Bend the spokes on the left to the right and behind the spoke on the right. Continue this second step all the way around the basket.

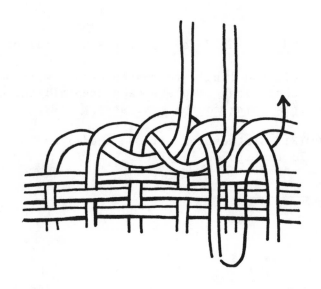

20. Place the upright spoke so that it rests against and follows the top of the curved spoke to its right, bringing the spoke back to the top side of the lip.

21. Place the spoke so that it rests against and on top of the spoke forming the bottom curve and is inserted to the underside of the lip.

22. When all four steps have been completed, cut off the excess lengths of the reeds on the underside of the lip. Leave enough length so that the reeds will not slip out of place.

TO FINISH THE SIDES:

23. Twine around the remaining upright spokes for six rounds or about 1".

24. Use the four-step method explained previously to finish the top of the basket.

TO MAKE THE LID:

The basket is shown with two lids. Depending upon the function of the basket, either lid may be chosen.

* * * * * * * * * * * *

A.   TO MAKE THE ROUNDED LID:

1. Cut 14 pieces of #2 round reed 30" long. These pieces of reed will be the spokes which will form the lid.

2. Place seven pieces of reed on top of the other seven pieces as shown in the illustration.

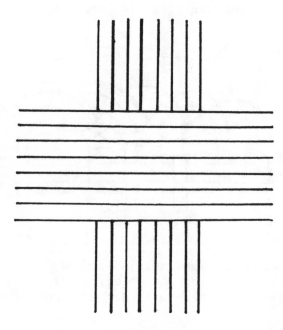

3. Using #2 round reed, twine around seven spokes at a time for two rounds.

4. Dampen all of the spokes.

5. Separate the seven spokes by bending them into sets of four, three, four, three, etc.

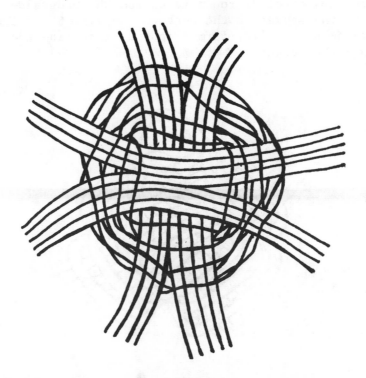

6. Twine around these sets of spokes for two rounds.

7. Separate the spokes again into four sets of two, two, one, two. Twine around these sets for two rounds.

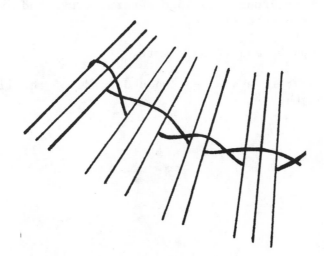

8. Twine around each individual spoke for six inches.

    NOTE: As you are twining, bend the spokes slightly to form the rounded shape.

9. Use the four-step method to finish the rim of the basket.

TO MAKE THE HANDLE:

10. Insert a piece of #2 round reed from the underside of the lid through the spokes in the center. Leaving 6" of the reed on the underside of the lid, form a loop by inserting the reed down through the spokes.

11. Bring the reed back to the top of the basket by inserting it into the same place it was started.

12. Wrap the reed around the loop several times and insert it back down and under the lid.

13. Repeat steps 11 and 12 once more.

14. Tie the reeds in a knot on the underside of the lid. Cut off any excess length.

B.   TO MAKE THE FLAT LID:

1.   Repeat steps 1 through 7 for the domed lid.

2.   Twine around each individual spoke for 5".

3.   Use the four-step method for finishing off the rim.

TO MAKE THE HANDLE:

4.   Insert a piece of #2 round reed from the underside of the lid through the spokes in the center.

5.   Leaving 6" on the underside of the lid, attach the knob by inserting the reed through the hole and back into the lid.

6.   Repeat this step once more and tie the reeds in a knot on the underside of the lid.   Cut off any excess length.

Variations of Wickerwork

Ribbed Baskets

HELPFUL SUGGESTIONS FOR RIBBED BASKETS

1. The bundles of reeds are referred to as hanks. Once a hank of reed is broken, it becomes difficult to handle. Because it is impractical to retie the hanks each time a few reeds are needed, a good method of storage is necessary. Plastic trash bags and old pillow cases are ideal for this purpose.

2. Do not oversoak the reeds. Too much soaking will cause the reeds to breakdown and become frayed. Flat reed will vary in thickness. Thin reeds are more pliable and require little dampness. Thicker reeds will need to be immersed in water. Blot the excess water with a towel.

3. Do not remove any length from the ribs when sharpening the ends.

4. When the distance between the original ribs is more than 2", secondary ribs must be added. Always add two secondary ribs between the original ribs so that the weaving will not be irregular.

5. Do not splice new weavers so that they will be doubled going over the rim.

6. If a rib should break, insert an ice pick or a knitting needle through the weavers and remove the broken rib. The needle will hold the weavers in place while inserting the new rib. Do this on both sides of the basket.

7. If the basket becomes wet for any reason, the hoops may come unglued and spring apart at the seams.

POTATO BASKET

The potato basket was used for harvesting potatoes. The handles on each side made it easy to carry.

Because the original baskets were made with splits from hardwood, such as oak, they were much stronger. The basket shown is made from commercial reed and may be used in a variety of ways.

POTATO BASKET

Materials:
    1/4" flat reed
    1/2" flat reed
    #6 round reed
    12" wooden hoop

TO MAKE THE FRAME:

1. Cut a piece of 1/2" flat reed to fit inside the circumference of the 12" hoop. Overlap the ends. Use clothespins to hold the reed in place.

2. Find the circumference of the hoop. Divide this figure in half in order to find the midpoints of the hoop. Mark these points.

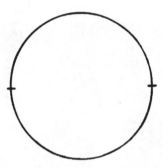

3. Cut three ribs 24" long using the #6 round reed. Using a knife, whittle the ends of the ribs so that each end has two flat sides, approximately 1/2" long.

    NOTE: Some round reeds come in coils rather than in straight lengths and will be curved. To prevent having to reshape the ribs, whittle the ends on the inside and the outside of the curve as shown in the following illustration. If the ribs are cut from round reed which has been packaged in straight lengths, it does not matter where the cuts are made as long as they are on opposite sides of the reed.

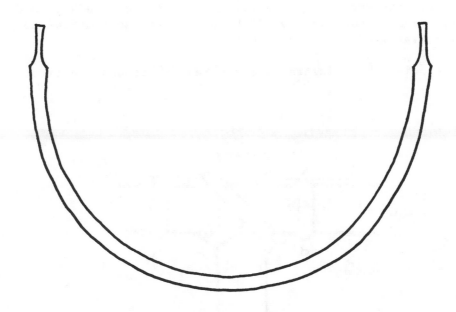

4. Insert the three 24" pieces of round reed between the hoop and the flat reed. Put the middle rib at the center mark and place the other ribs on either side with approximately one inch separating them. Hold the ribs in place with clothespins.

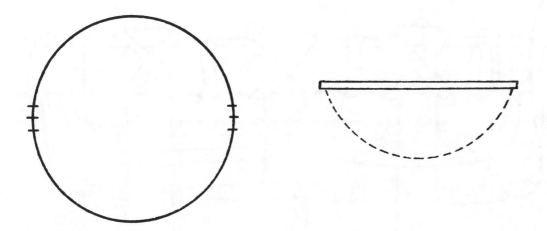

TO LASH THE RIBS IN PLACE:

5. Wet a piece of 1/4" flat reed and cut the width in half lengthwise to make two 1/8" pieces of reed.

6. Insert the end of the 1/8" flat reed between the hoop and the flat reed. Loop it around the entire rim so that the hoop and flat reed are tied together.

7. Following the illustration, make an "X" around the first rib.

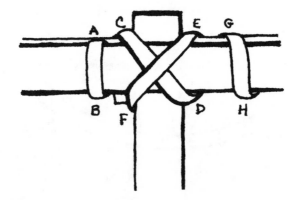

8. Repeat these steps for the other two ribs.

> NOTE: Be sure to make the loop between each rib.

> NOTE: Do not cut off the excess reed as it will be used to weave around the ribs. Use a clothespin to secure the reed to the rim.

9. Repeat the entire procedure on the three ribs on the opposite side of the basket.

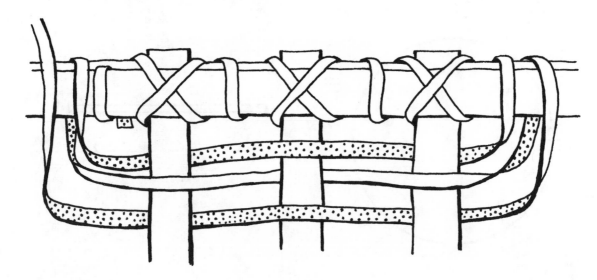

TO BEGIN WEAVING:

10. Begin weaving the basket by following the pattern shown in the illustration which follows step nine.

> NOTE: Dampen all of the weavers for flexibility and to prevent breakage.

> NOTE: Alternate weaving on each side of the basket so that it will maintain a good shape.

11. When coming to the end of a weaver, overlap it with another one and weave the two as one for several ribs, hiding the ends as much as possible. This procedure is called splicing.

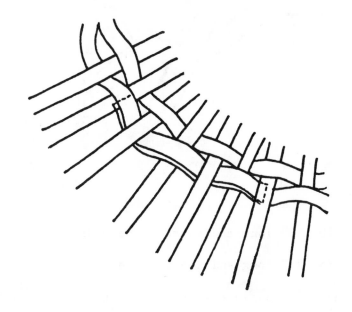

149

12. Continue weaving until there is enough room to insert more ribs.

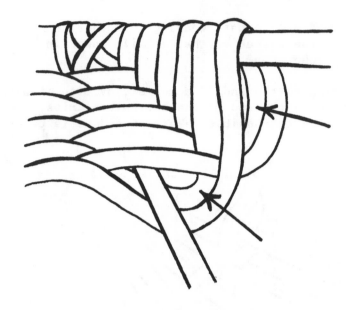

13. Cut two ribs 20" long and sharpen the ends.

14. Cut two ribs 21" long and sharpen the ends.

15. Insert the 20" ribs in the space next to the rim on both sides of the basket.

16. Insert the 21" ribs in the space formed next to the 24" ribs on both sides of the basket.

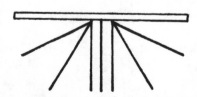

17. Continue weaving until there is room to insert more ribs.

18. Add two ribs between the 24" rib and the 21" rib on each side of the basket.

19. Add two ribs between the 21" rib and the 20" rib on each side.

20. Insert two ribs on each side of the basket next to the rim.

> NOTE: The lengths of these ribs will vary, but each will be close in length to the ribs they are placed beside of.

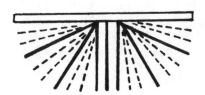

21. When the rim has only 4" of unwoven space on both sides of the basket, begin to weave over the rib next to the rim (instead of weaving over the rim) and back down.

This will create a space between the rim and the rib which serves as a handle. Do this on both sides of the basket.

TO FINISH THE HANDLE:

22. Wet a piece of 1/4" flat reed and insert the end under the weavers at the rim. Wrap the reed closely around the exposed handle, inserting the end under the weavers on the other side.

151

SCOTTISH HEN BASKET

The design of the Scottish Hen Basket, narrow at the top and wide at the bottom, was convenient for carrying hens from place to place. The shape of the handle made the basket easy to carry on one's arm. The design was found to be so convenient to use that women later used these baskets as pocketbooks. There are many practical uses for a basket of this type.

SCOTTISH HEN BASKET

Materials:
    1 12" hoop (7/16" wide)
    2 7" hoops (7/16" wide)
    #2 round reed
    #6 round reed
    1/4" flat reed

TO MAKE THE FRAME:

1. Soak several long strands of #2 round reed in water for about
    five minutes.

2. Place a 7" hoop on each side of the 12" hoop.

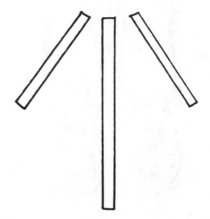

3. Place the end of one strand of #2 round reed under the 12"
    hoop. Bring the reed over the top of one 7" hoop. Wrap it
    around and under the hoop so that it can then be brought back
    over the top of the 12" hoop. Go under the 7" hoop on the
    other side. Wrap the reed around and over the top of the
    hoop so that it can then be brought back under the 12" hoop.
    Repeat this pattern until the three hoops are held together
    by the round reed. This should be accomplished after four or
    five rounds.

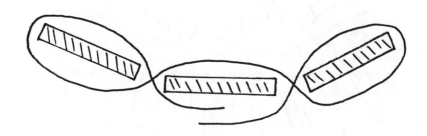

4. To assure that the bottom will be wide enough, hold the 7" hoops out as you continue to weave the handle.

> NOTE: As you weave, the 7" hoops have a tendency to be pulled close together at the bottom. To prevent losing the necessary fullness, hold the 12" hoop between your knees and rest the 7" hoops on top of your legs.

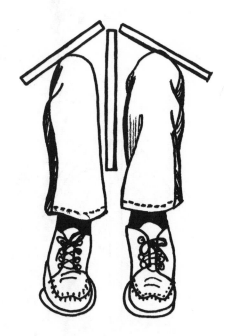

5. Continue weaving down the sides of the handles until the distance is the same on both sides for a total of seven inches. Weaving must be alternated on each side of the handle to accomplish this.

6. When coming to the end of a weaver, overlap it with another reed and weave the two as one for several ribs. Hide the ends of the weavers as much as possible. This procedure is called splicing.

7. Cut two pieces of #6 round reed 34" long.

8. Cut two pieces of #6 round reed 32" long.

9. Using a knife or pencil sharpener, sharpen each end of each rib to a point. Be careful not to remove any of the length of the ribs.

TO INSERT THE RIBS:

10. Insert the ribs, as shown in the illustration, putting one end of each rib into each side of the handle. These ribs will follow the same curve as the 7" hoops.

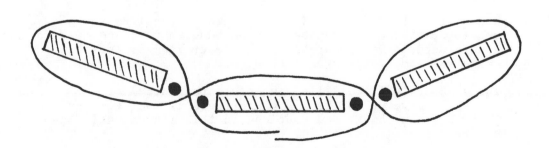

TO WEAVE THE BASKET:

NOTE: Dampen all of the weavers to be used
for flexibility and to prevent breakage.

NOTE: The pattern used for the weaving will
be over one, under one, including all three
hoops in the weaving pattern.

11. Using two pieces of #2 round reed as one, continue weaving
down both sides of the basket. Weave this double pattern for
about two inches.

12. Using #6 round reed, cut two each of the following lengths:

24", 18".

Using #6 round reed, cut four each of the following lengths:

30", 29".

13. Insert these ribs as shown in the illustration.

14. Using a single strand of #2 round reed, weave over one and
under one for a couple of inches on each side of the basket.

15. At this point you may wish to add more ribs. If so, the
length will be determined by the shape of your basket.

16. A weaver of 1/4" flat reed may be used to continue the
weaving pattern. It may be alternated with #2 round reed for
a more decorative appearance. Whichever reed is chosen,
weave the same pattern on each side.

17. The 7" hoops will be filled in before the bottom of the
basket. Weave up to the rib where there is room to continue
going over and back, and continue in this manner until the
entire basket is filled in.

OVAL KEY BASKET

The key basket was usually found hanging near an outside door. It was a convenient place for holding keys to outbuildings and storage rooms.

OVAL KEY BASKET

Materials:
    2 hoops (oval, 4" x 9")   1/4" flat or flat oval reed
    1 dowel (4" long)   2 small nails
    #5 round reed

TO MAKE THE FRAME:

1. Cut one of the hoops in half.

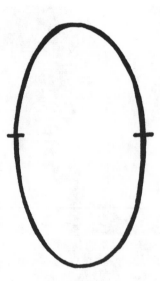

2. Place one half of the oval hoop on the outside of the whole oval hoop a little above the center.

3. Place the dowel on the inside of the oval hoop in the same place as above.

4. Drive a nail through the half hoop into the whole hoop and the dowel.

5. Repeat step four on the other side of the basket.

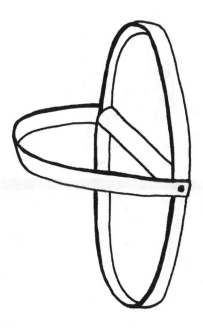

TO MAKE THE GOD'S EYE:

6. Select two of the longest pieces of 1/4" flat reed available to make the God's Eyes. These reeds should be dampened.

7. Hiding the end of one reed on the inside of the frame where the hoops have been joined, weave the God's Eyes as shown in the illustration. At step 9, you are beginning the second round. Continue going around the hoops until five complete rounds have been formed. Weave more than five rounds, if necessary, to form the spaces for inserting the ribs.

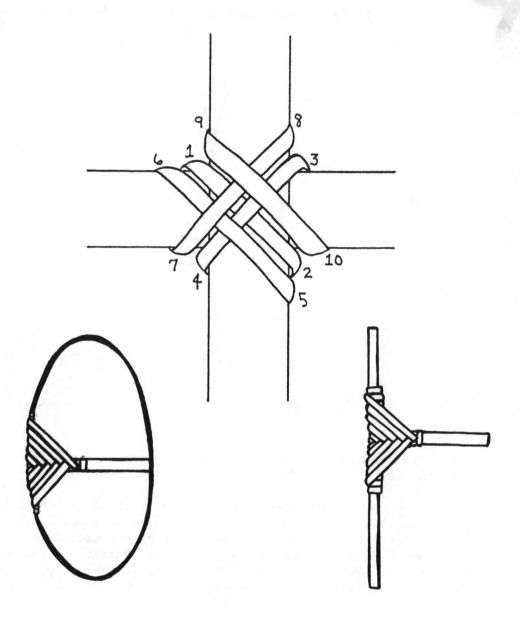

NOTE: Do not cut off the excess reed as
it will be used to weave around the ribs
after they have been inserted. A clothespin
can be used to secure the excess reed and
keep the God's Eye from unraveling.

8. Repeat step seven to form the God's Eye on the other side of the
basket.

TO MAKE THE RIBS:

9. Using #5 round reed, cut one each of the following lengths:

    10 1/2", 13 1/4", 15 3/4", 17", 15 1/4", 13 1/4"

10. Using #5 round reed, cut one each of the following lengths:

    5 1/2", 5 1/2", 8 1/2", 10 3/4"

11. Using a knife or pencil sharpener, sharpen each end of each rib to a point. Be careful not to take off any of the length of the ribs.

TO INSERT THE RIBS:

12. The ends of the ribs will be hidden behind the God's Eye on the inside of the basket as shown in the illustration which follows.

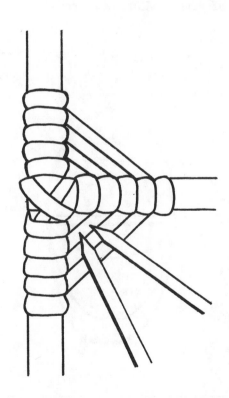

13. Begin inserting the ribs by placing the 15 3/4" rib next to the rim on the front of the basket

14. Insert the 17" rib just below the 15 3/4" rib.

15. On the back of the basket, insert the 5 1/2" rib next to the rim.

16. Insert the 10 3/4" rib below the 5 1/2" rib.

NOTE: At this pont, the only security these ribs have is from the pressure exerted by the ribs being bent and placed in the frame.

TO BEGIN WEAVING:

>NOTE: The pattern used for the weaving
>will be over one, under one. Weave both
>the front and the back of the basket,
>including the rims and the frame at the
>bottom of the basket.

>NOTE: Dampen all of the weavers to be
>used for flexibility and to prevent
>breakage.

17. To begin weaving, be sure that the God's Eye has ended so
that the flat reed is coming out from the inside of the
basket between the rim and the first rib. Weave over one rib
and under one rib until the weaver ends.

18. Repeat the step above using the excess flat reed on the other
side of the basket.

>NOTE: Alternate weaving on each side of
>the basket in order to maintain the correct
>shape.

19. When coming to the end of a weaver, overlap it with another
reed and weave the two as one for several ribs. Hide the
ends of the weavers as much as possible. This procedure is
called splicing.

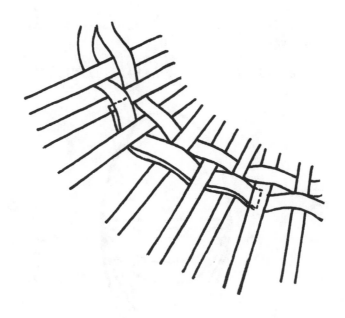

20. Continue weaving until there is room to add the other ribs.

21. Insert the 10 1/2" rib between the front rim and the 15 3/4" rib.

22. Insert the 13 1/4" rib between the 10 1/2" rib and the 15 3/4" rib.

23. Insert the 15 1/4" rib between the 17" rib and the frame at the bottom of the basket.

24. Insert the other 13 1/4" rib between the 15 1/4" rib and the frame.

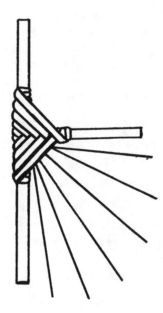

25. On the back, insert the 5 1/2" rib between the 5 1/2" rib and the 10 3/4" rib.

26. Insert the 8 1/2" rib between the 5 1/2" rib and the 10 3/4" rib.

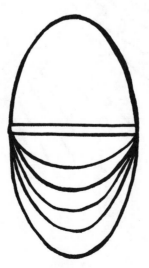

27. Continue weaving. The rim may fill up before the bottom of the basket. If it does, weave up to the rib where there is room to continue going over and back.

28. Continue weaving until the basket is completely filled in.

TO FINISH THE HANDLE:

Two methods may be used for finishing the handles:

A. Using a long piece of 1/4" flat reed, dampen it and place the end under the reeds on the handle which form the God's Eye. Wrap the reed around the handle, placing each round close together. Once the handle is covered, hide the end of the reed under the God's Eye on the other side of the basket.

B. This is a variation of method A. You will need two pieces of 1/4" flat reed. Cut one piece a little longer than the length of the exposed handle. Dampen a long piece of flat reed and insert one end into the God's Eye on one side of the basket. Place the shorter piece of flat reed on top of the handle. Wrap the long piece twice around the handle and the short reed. Wrap the long reed around the handle two more times, going between the short reed and the handle. This will leave the short piece exposed. Wrap the long reed twice more around the handle and the short reed. Continue alternating this pattern until the handle is covered. Insert the ends into the God's Eye on the other side of the basket.

You can establish your own variations by changing the number of times you wrap over and under the handle and the short reed.

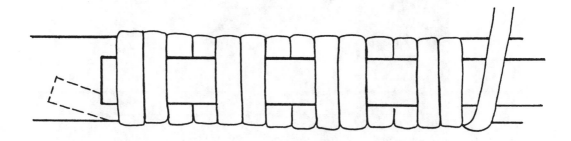

MEASUREMENTS FOR A 10" ROUND KEY BASKET

Materials Needed:
   2 10" hoops
   1 dowel (9 1/2" long)
   #6 round reed
   1/4" flat or flat oval reed
   2 small nails

   Ribs for the front of the basket:

         13", 14", 17", 15 1/2", 15 1/2", 19", 15", 14"

   Ribs for the back of the basket:

         10", 8 1/2", 11", 12"

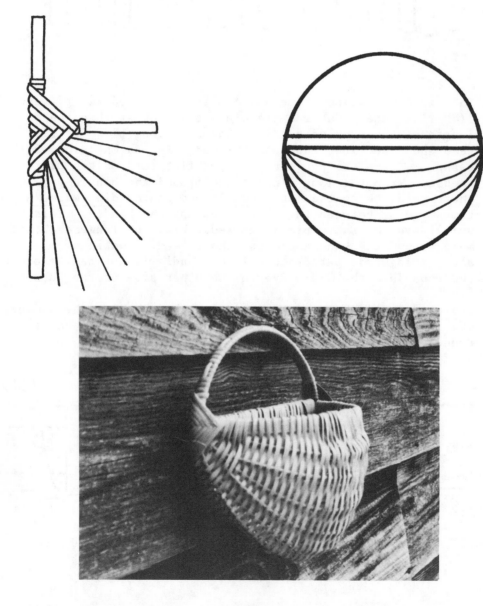

KEY BASKET WITH GRAPEVINE FRAME

After making the oval key basket, this variation will be easy to complete. The grapevine key basket allows the basketmaker more creativity as a result of the materials used.

KEY BASKET WITH GRAPEVINE FRAME

Materials:
    Grapevine
    #6 round reed
    #2 round reed
    1/4" flat or flat oval reed

TO MAKE THE FRAME:

1. Grapevine to be used in this basket may be gathered in the late fall or winter. The size can vary. For this basket, grapevine with a diameter somewhere between the size of a pencil and one's little finger would be most suitable.

2. Take a piece of grapevine 10' long and form a circle which has a diameter of approximately 10" by wrapping the grapevine in and around itself. The circumference of this part of the frame should be about 40".

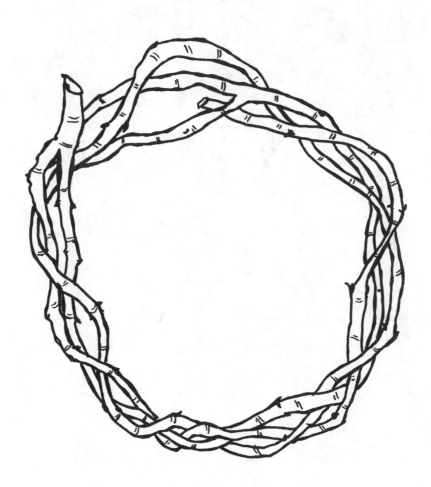

3. Cut a 17" piece of grapevine which is as straight as
   possible. Use string to tie this length of grapevine to the
   circle a little above the center on both sides. Allow the
   ends to stick out beyond the circle. This will form the rim
   on the back of the basket.

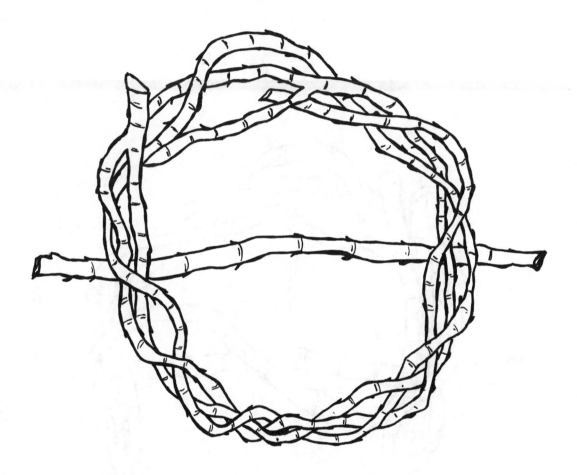

4. Cut a piece of grapevine 28" long. This will be used to form
   the rim on the front of the basket. Use string to attach the
   rim to both sides of the frame at the same points where the
   back rim has been attached.

Be sure to place the curved rim so that it will not lie flat against the back, but will form a pocket.

> NOTE: The front rim must be curved. To achieve this, one end of the grapevine must be turned up at the point where it is attached to the frame. On the other side of the basket, the end of the grapevine must be turned down.

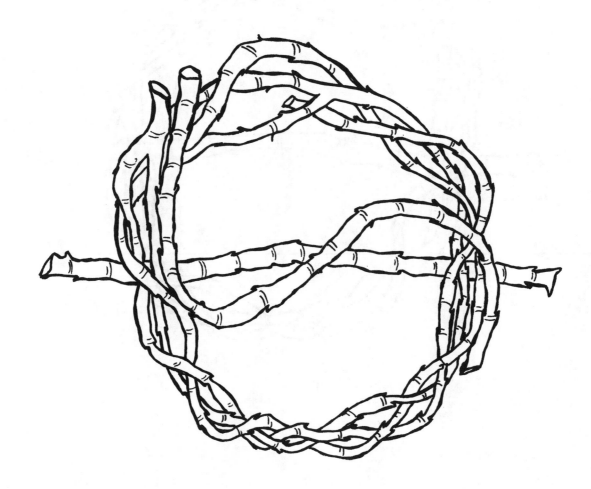

5. Dampen a piece of 1/4" flat reed or #2 round reed. Form a God's Eye on each side of the basket at the point where the frame is tied together. The God's Eye in this basket will not be wrapped around the back rim. After completing the God's Eye, cut off the excess reed and secure the ends by tucking them into the frame.

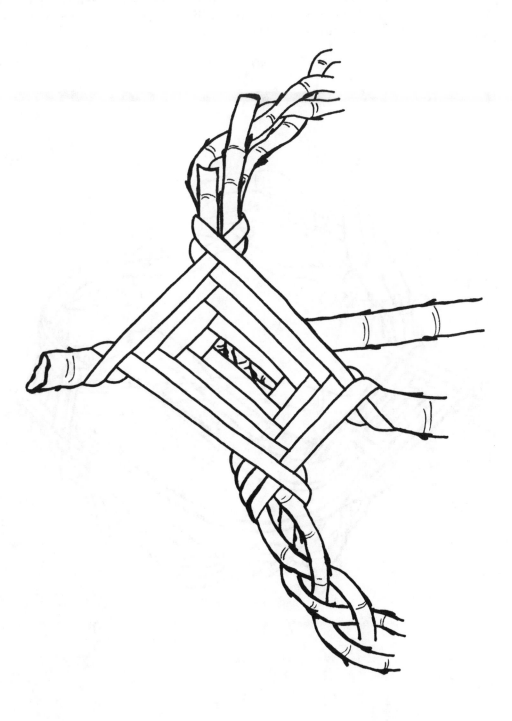

6. The ribs of the basket will be secured at the God's Eyes.
   The lengths of the ribs will be determined by the shape of
   the grapevine. Try to follow the natural curves of the
   frame. Using #6 round reed, begin by inserting two or three
   ribs on the front and two on the back. The longer the ribs
   on the front are, the fuller the basket will be.

   The rib immediately under the rim on the front should follow
   the same curve as the rim. The rib on the bottom should
   follow the same curve as the bottom of the frame.

FRONT VIEW

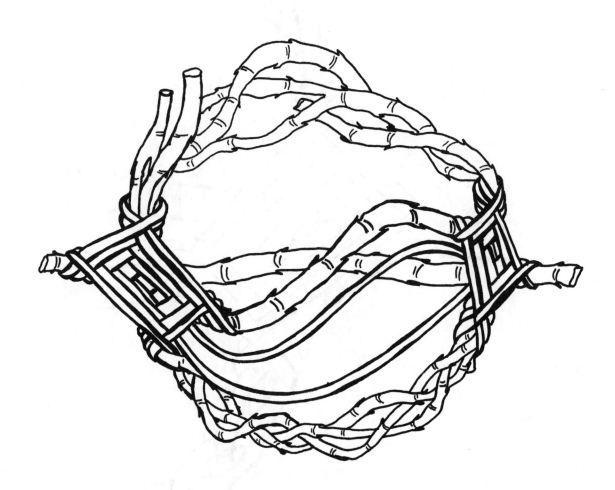

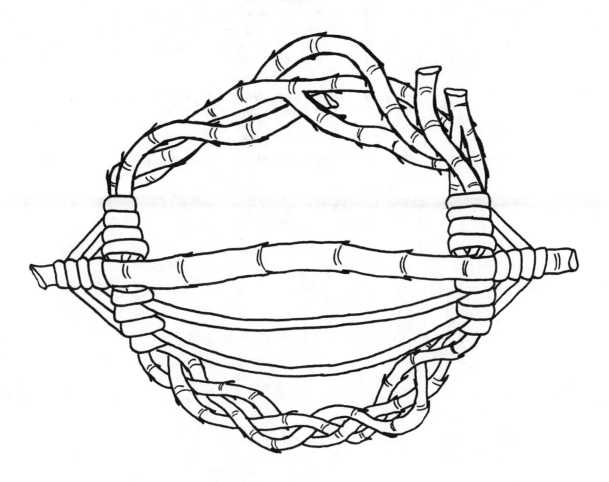

7. The pattern for weaving will be over one, under one. Weave both the front and the back, including the rims and the frame at the bottom of the basket.

> NOTE: Alternate weaving on each side of the basket in order to have the correct shape when the basket is finished.

8. Using 1/4" flat reed, hide the end in the God's Eye and weave
    down each side until there is room to add more ribs. The
    lengths of the ribs will vary. To prevent a noticeable
    change in the pattern, be sure to add two ribs between each
    original pair of ribs.

9. The rim may fill up before the bottom of the basket. If it
    does, weave up to the rib where there is room to continue
    going over and back.

10. Continue weaving until the basket is completely filled in.

>   NOTE: The string used for holding the
>   grapevine in place may be cut out when
>   the basket has been completed.

EGG BASKET

The egg basket was used for carrying eggs. Its
unusual shape helped prevent the eggs from rolling around and
breaking.

EGG BASKET

Materials:
- 2 7" hoops (3/8" wide)
- #5 round reed
- 1/4" flat or flat oval reed

TO MAKE THE FRAME:

1. Find the seam of one hoop and mark it with an "X".

2. Using a tape measure, find the circumference of the hoop. Divide this figure in half in order to find the midpoints of the hoop. Mark these points on the hoop making sure they are not near the seam.

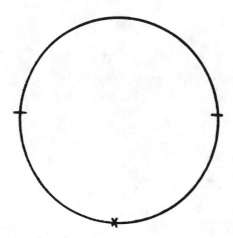

3. Four notches will be made at each midpoint, two on each side of the hoop. Using the midpoint as the center, there should be 3/8" between each pair of notches.

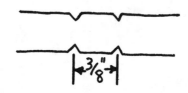

4. Repeat step 3 at the opposite midpoint.

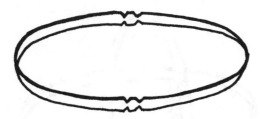

5. Find the seam on the second hoop and mark it with an "X" as you did before.

6. Directly opposite the seam, mark the hoop with an "H". This will designate this hoop as the handle.

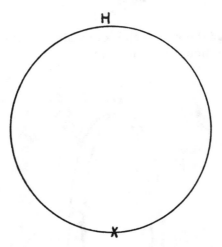

7. The exposed handle will be 10" in length. Measure 10" using the "H" as the center. Mark these points.

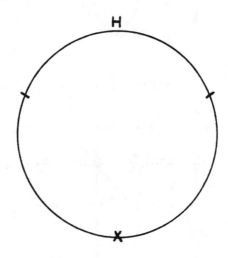

8. Four notches will be made at each point, two on each side of the hoop. Notch these points in the same manner as you did the first hoop.

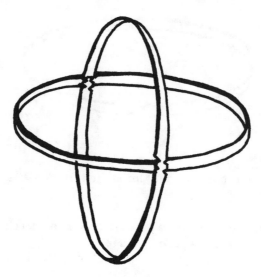

9. Place the second hoop on the outside of the first hoop with the notches on each hoop matched up.

10. Using strong cord, tie the hoops together on both sides of the frame.

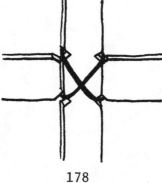

VARIATIONS OF FINISHING HANDLES:

The handle of a basket may be left plain or made decorative by
using any of several methods available to the basketmaker.

> NOTE: Method C and the attaching of the
> decorative rim must be done before the God's
> Eyes are made. Methods A and B may be done
> after the God's Eyes are made, or when the
> basket is completed.

A. The following is the easiest method for finishing a handle.
Dampen a long piece of 1/4" flat reed and place the end under the
reeds on the handle which form the God's Eye. Wrap the reed
around the handle, placing each round closely together. Once the
handle is covered, hide the end of the reed under the God's Eye
on the other side of the basket.

B. This is a variation of Method A. You will need two pieces of
flat reed. Cut a piece of 1/4" flat reed a little longer than
the length of the exposed handle. Dampen a long piece of flat
reed and insert it into the reeds which form the God's Eye on one
side of the basket. Place the shorter piece of flat reed on top
of the handle. Wrap the long piece twice around the handle and
the short piece of reed. Wrap the long piece around the handle
two more times, going between the short reed and the handle.
This will leave the short reed exposed. Wrap the reed twice more
around the handle and the short reed. Continue alternating this
pattern until the handle is covered. Insert the ends into the
reeds which form the God's Eye on the side of the basket.

You can establish your own variations by changing the number of
times you wrap over and under the handle and the short reed.

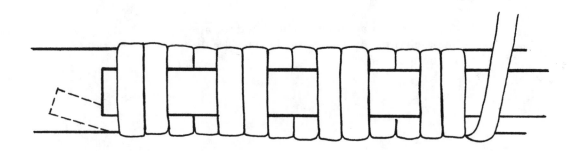

C. This method is the most complicated and must be done before the God's Eyes are made. This method will increase the width of the handle.

Using the same round reed which will be used for the ribs, cut two pieces which are longer than the handle. The ends of these reeds may be secured on both sides of the basket with masking tape which will be hidden under the God's Eyes.

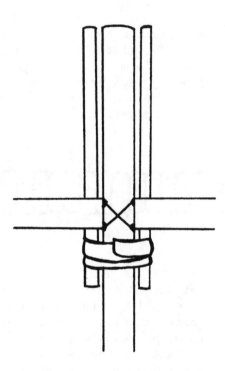

NOTE: If the decorative rim will be used, it must be added at this point. Directions for the rim follow this method of finishing the handle.

After securing the ribs, make the God's Eyes on either side of the basket.

NOTE: You may weave the handle at this point, or wait until the basket is completed.

TO WEAVE THE HANDLE:

Dampen a long piece of 1/4" flat reed and place the end under the reeds which form the God's Eyes on one side of the basket. The pattern for weaving the handle is over one, under one, as shown in the following illustration.

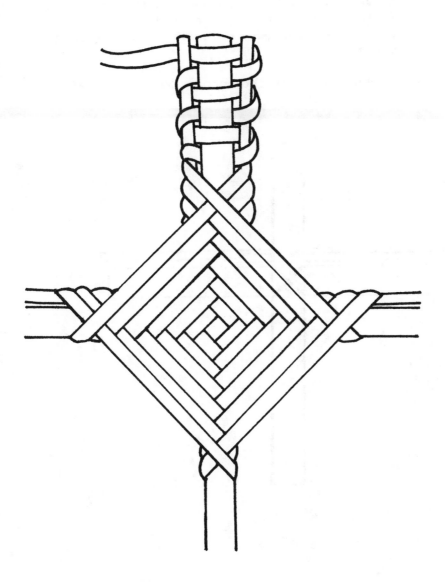

After the handle has been completely filled in, insert the end under the God's Eye.

OPTIONAL DECORATIVE RIM:

After the hoops have been joined, the decorative rim will be attached. Using the same size round reed that will be used for the ribs, form a circle slightly larger than the hoop which forms the rim.

Place the decorative rim on top of the hoop so that the ends which overlap are behind the handle on one side. This reed should be secured with masking tape which will be covered by making the God's Eye.

Be sure to weave over and under the decorative rim as well as the ribs and hoop of the basket.

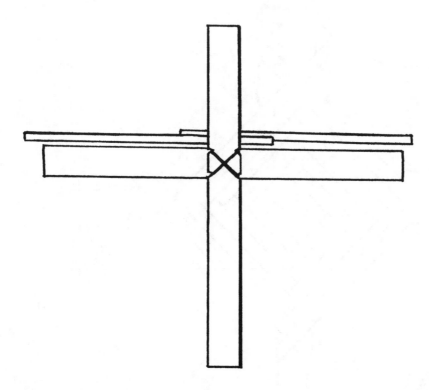

TO MAKE THE GOD'S EYE:

11. Select two of the longest pieces of 1/4" flat reed available to make the God's Eyes. These reeds should be dampened.

12. Hiding the end of one reed on the inside of the frame where the hoops have been joined, weave the God's Eyes as shown in the illustration. At step 9, you are beginning the second round. Continue going around the hoops until six complete rounds have been formed.

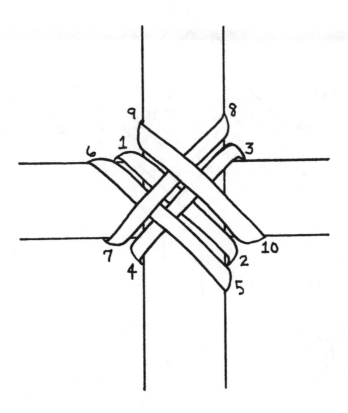

NOTE: Do not cut off the excess reed as it will be used to weave around the ribs after they have been inserted. A clothespin can be used to secure the excess reed and keep the God's Eye from unraveling.

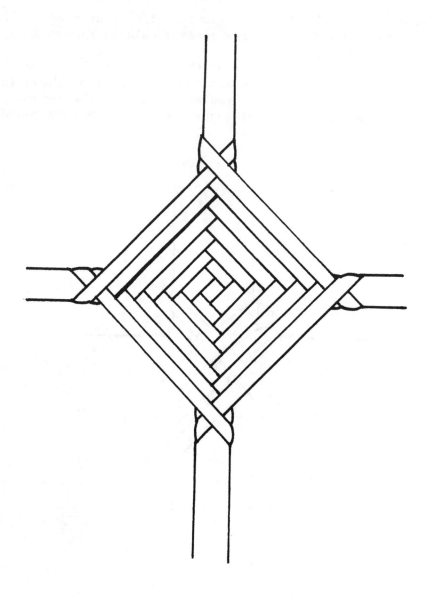

13. Repeat steps eleven and twelve to make the God's Eye on the other side of the frame.

TO MAKE THE RIBS:

14. Using #5 round reed, cut two pieces of each of the following lengths:

    12 1/2", 14 1/2", 15 1/2", 15", 13"

    NOTE: Because the lengths of the ribs are so similar, marking them will eliminate measuring each one as you place it in the frame.

15. Mark the 12 1/2" ribs with one dot.

16. Mark the 14 1/2" ribs with two dots.

17. Mark the 15 1/2" ribs with three dots.

18. Mark the 15" ribs with four dots.

19. Mark the 13" ribs with five dots.

20. Using a knife or pencil sharpener, sharpen each end of each rib to a point. Be careful not to take off any of the length of the ribs.

TO INSERT THE RIBS:

21. One rib of each length will be placed on each side of the basket. The ends of the ribs will be hidden behind the God's Eyes.

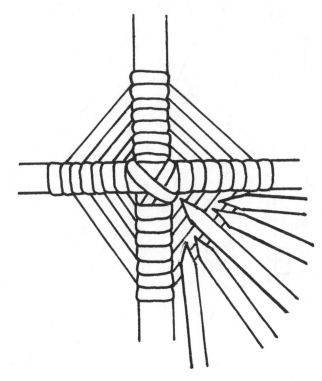

22. The ribs will be placed into the frame of the basket in sequence beginning with the "one dot" ribs and ending with the "five dot" ribs.

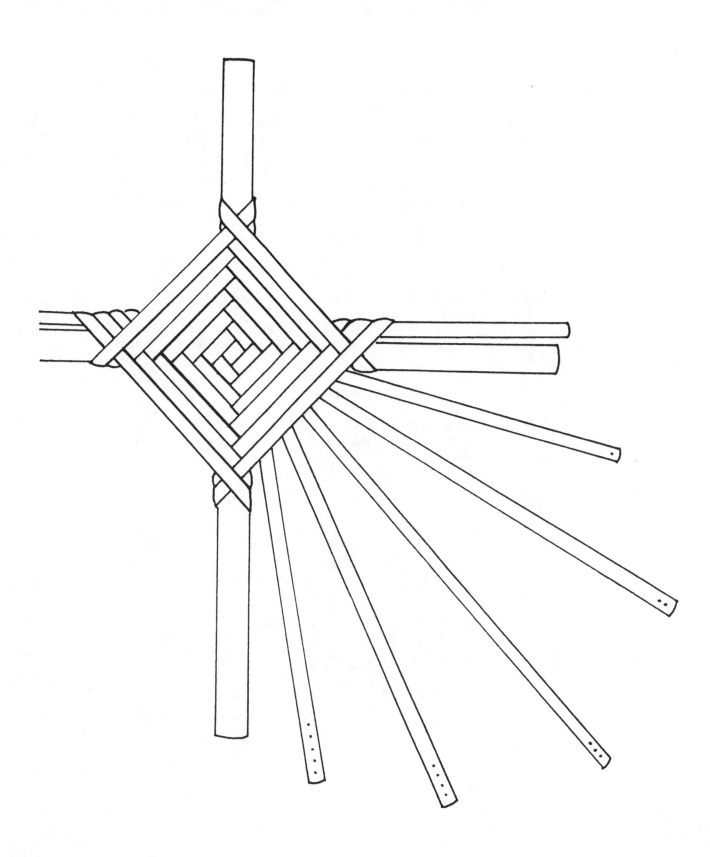

NOTE: At this point, the only security
these ribs have is from the pressure
exerted by the ribs being bent and placed
in the frame. The ribs will pop out of
place until a few rounds of weaving have
been completed on both sides of the
basket.

NOTE: So that the shape of the basket
will not be altered, the ends of the
ribs should be arranged exactly as shown
in the illustration which follows Step
21.

TO BEGIN WEAVING:

> NOTE: The pattern used for the weaving
> will be over one, under one. Weave both
> the front and the back of the basket,
> including the rims and the frame at the
> bottom of the basket.

> NOTE: Dampen all of the weavers to be
> used for flexibility and to prevent
> breakage.

23. To begin weaving, be sure that the God's Eye has ended so
    that the flat reed is coming out from the inside of the
    basket between the rim and the first rib. Weave over one rib
    and under one rib until the weaver ends.

24. Repeat the step above using the excess flat reed on the other
    side of the basket.

    > NOTE: Alternate weaving on each side of
    > the basket in order to maintain the correct
    > shape.

25. When coming to the end of a weaver, overlap it with another
    reed and weave the two as one for several inches. Hide the
    ends of the weavers as much as possible. This procedure is
    called splicing.

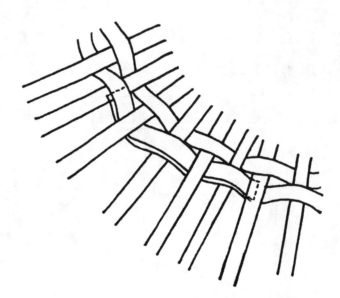

26. The rim may fill up before the bottom of the basket. If it
    does, weave up to the rib where there is room to continue
    going over and back. Continue in this manner until the
    entire basket is filled in.

MEASUREMENTS FOR EGG AND MELON BASKETS

A melon basket is made using the same procedure as an egg basket. The melon basket, which was used for marketing, has a more rounded bottom.

The larger egg baskets will be sturdier and more attractive if more than the five original ribs are used. When adding these secondary ribs, always put two ribs between the original ribs so that the pattern will not change noticeably.

The lengths of these secondary ribs will vary, but each will be close in length to the ribs they are placed beside of.

It will not be necessary to add secondary ribs between all of the original ribs. A general rule would be to add the secondary ribs if the space between the original ribs is more than 2".

Cut two ribs for each measurement from the size of round reed which is indicated. The numbers 1 through 5 to the left show the order of placement in the basket.

3" Egg Basket	3" Melon Basket
4 1/2" Handle	4 1/2" Handle
#5 round reed	#5 round reed
1 - 5"	1 - 4 3/4"
2 - 5 3/4"	2 - 5"
3 - 6"	3 - 5 1/2"
4 - 5 1/2"	4 - 5 1/4"
5 - 5 1/4"	5 - 5"

4" Egg Basket	4" Melon Basket
6" Handle	6" Handle
#5 round reed	#5 round reed
1 - 6 3/4"	1 - 6 1/4"
2 - 8 1/4"	2 - 6 1/2"
3 - 10"	3 - 7"
4 - 8 1/2"	4 - 6 3/4"
5 - 7"	5 - 6 1/2"

5" Egg Basket	5" Melon Basket
7" Handle	7" Handle
#5 round reed	#5 round reed
1 - 9"	1 - 7 1/4"
2 - 10 1/2"	2 - 7 1/2"
3 - 11"	3 - 8"
4 - 10 3/4"	4 - 7 3/4"
5 - 9"	5 - 7 1/2"

6" Egg Basket
9" Handle
#6 round reed
1 - 9 1/2"
2 - 11"
3 - 12"
4 - 11 1/2"
5 - 10"

6" Melon Basket
9" Handle
#6 round reed
1 - 8 3/4"
2 - 9 1/2"
3 - 10 1/4"
4 - 9 1/2"
5 - 9 1/4"

7" Egg Basket
10" Handle
#6 round reed
1 - 12 1/2"
2 - 14 1/2"
3 - 15 1/2"
4 - 15"
5 - 13"

7" Melon Basket
10" Handle
#6 round reed
1 - 11 1/2"
2 - 12"
3 - 12 1/2"
4 - 12 1/2"
5 - 12"

8" Egg Basket
12" Handle
#6 round reed
1 - 13 1/2"
2 - 15 1/2"
3 - 18 1/2"
4 - 16 1/2"
5 - 14 1/2"

8" Melon Basket
12" Handle
#6 round reed
1 - 11 1/2"
2 - 12"
3 - 13"
4 - 13"
5 - 12 1/2"

10" Egg Basket
14" Handle
#7 round reed
1 - 16"
2 - 19"
3 - 21 1/2"
4 - 21 1/2"
5 - 19"

10" Melon Basket
14" Handle
#7 round reed
1 - 16 1/2"
2 - 18"
3 - 19"
4 - 19"
5 - 17 1/2"

12" Egg Basket
17 1/2" Handle
#7 round reed
1 - 20"
2 - 23"
3 - 24 1/2"
4 - 23 1/2"
5 - 21"

12" Melon Basket
17 1/2" Handle
#7 round reed
1 - 19"
2 - 20"
3 - 21"
4 - 21"
5 - 20"

14" Egg Basket
17" Handle
#7 round reed
1 - 24 1/2"
2 - 27"
3 - 30"
4 - 28"
5 - 24 1/2"

14" Melon Basket
17" Handle
#7 round reed
1 - 21"
2 - 22"
3 - 24"
4 - 24"
5 - 23 1/2"

18" Egg Basket
25 3/4" Handle
#8 round reed
1 - 29"
2 - 35"
3 - 41 1/2"
4 - 38 1/2"
5 - 31 1/2"

18" Melon Basket
25 3/4" Handle
#8 round reed
1 - 29"
2 - 31"
3 - 33"
4 - 33"
5 - 29 3/4"

23" Egg Basket
33" Handle
#8 round reed
1 - 37"
2 - 40"
3 - 44"
4 - 40 1/2"
5 - 39"

23" Melon Basket
33" Handle
#8 round reed
1 - 34 1/2"
2 - 37"
3 - 36 1/2"
4 - 36 1/2"
5 - 36 1/2"

Variations of Ribbed Baskets